THE MASONIC WHY
AND WHEREFORE

(Being Answers to 101
Questions which perplex
the average Mason)

BY

W. BRO. J. S. M. WARD,
M.A., P.M., P.Z., P.M.W.S.

THE BASKERVILLE PRESS, LIMITED
161, NEW BOND STREET, LONDON, W.1.

Printing Statement:

Due to the very old age and scarcity of this book,
many of the pages may be hard to read due to the
blurring of the original text, possible missing pages,
missing text and other issues beyond our control.

Because this is such an important and rare work, we
believe it is best to reproduce this book regardless of
its original condition.

Thank you for your understanding.

CONTENTS.

ILLUSTRATIONS.

AN EGYPTIAN VIGNETTE SHOWING HOW THE ANCIENT EGYPTIANS
EXPRESSED THEIR SORROW AND SYMPATHY AT A FUNERAL.

INTRODUCTION.

Having received a number of requests from brethren for a compact little book which will enable them to answer the questions of enquiring younger brethren, I have been moved to bring out this small work. It is arranged as a series of 101 Questions and Answers, the questions being chosen because in practically every instance they have at some time been asked me by one or more brethren.

Such a book, I believe, will be handy and useful, but of course it has its limitations, for in a brief and concise answer it is impossible to set out all the reasons and proofs which have led me to certain conclusions. Therefore brethren who are inclined to disagree with some of the answers or who feel that they would like to obtain more detailed information on the subject, should turn to some of my longer and fuller works.

In conclusion it is my sincere hope that some of the younger brethren after reading this book may be led to a more detailed study of the history and symbolism of our noble Order.

J. S. M. WARD.

Jan., 1929.

The Masonic Why and Wherefore.

CHAPTER I.

THE E.A. DEGREE.

1. Why is the Cand. deprived of M...ls before Entering?

M...ls are supposed to be the gift of the Gods of the Underworld, who are hostile to the Gods of Light. Freemasonry is essentially a Solar Cult and this prejudice against the use of m...ls in connection with religious observances is nearly always associated with the worship of the benign Spirits of Light.

In ancient Egypt stone knives continued to be used by the embalmers when preparing the corpse long after metal knives had come into use in the everyday world.

The explanation given in the Lectures, namely, that m...ls are excluded because m...l tools were not used on the Site of King Solomon's Temple at Jerusalem, does not really help us, except so far as it is intended to convey the lesson that the cand. is a stone prepared for

the building of the Temple of Humanity.
Even if the tradition be true, as is quite
possible, the reason would be the same as that
previously given, and would be for the object
of excluding anything which might belong to
the gods of the Underworld.

There is, moreover, another probable explanation. In ancient days it was believed
that in the Mysteries, as part of the ceremony,
the Hierophant, or Master, passed a magnetic
current through the novice, and in the ceremony
of the Consecration of a Priest in the Christian
Church the same idea still holds sway. That
such a magnetic force can be conveyed is possible, although to-day it is rare, and any such
substance as   m...l tends to check it and
reduce its power, just in the same way as
it will divert an electric current.

That there is some such definite intention, or
rather a dim memory of such a belief, is shown
by the emphatic statement at the end of the
ceremony, that the presence of m...ls would
have completely invalidated it. The moment
at which this magnetic force was directed on the
cand. was apparently at the obligation, for the
manner of the preparation, which brings the
bare kn. near to Mother earth, indicates this
to be the crucial moment.

Knowledge of these facts having almost entirely died out, the presence of this peculiar

regulation must be due to a survival, and is one of the many indications both of the great antiquity of our Order and of its connection with the Ancient Mysteries.

* * *

2. Why is the Can. Prepared in such a Peculiar Manner?

There is little doubt that originally the ob. was taken at a cubical stone altar which stood in the centre of the building, and even to-day in the North of England a wooden substitute for this altar is used instead of the Master's ped.. Now in very ancient days it was customary to swear by the altar itself, the use of the Bible being comparatively modern, and even to-day among savages one of the most common forms of an oath is to place one hand on a rock and swear thereby.

In such cases it is essential that the naked flesh should come in contact with the stone, just as an Englishman takes off his gloves when about to shake hands. It will be noted that the parts made b. are just those which would come in contact with the stone altar. As to the b...ng of the k., besides touching the altar at the the ob., this would also come into contact with the ground and, in early days, with Mother earth, and so enable the magnetic current men tioned in Question I. to flow freely.

With regard to the emphasis laid on the left side generally, in symbolism this side is supposed to be feminine because with most men it is the weaker side, and the association with the feminine and birth is fairly obvious.

*   *   *

3.   Why is the Cand. Sl.. Sh.d ?

In the Scotch ritual we are definitely told that this is in allusion to the custom among the Hebrews of sealing a bargain, as in the case of Boaz and Ruth, and it is possible that there may also be a reference to the fact that we are treading on holy ground.   But if this were all one would expect both s..s to be removed, for it must be noted that the cand. is sl.p s..d, not b..e f..t.d, and it is the latter which is the correct procedure when entering an Eastern Temple.   We find, however, that in many parts of the world there was an ancient superstitition that it was wise to remove one shoe when in any great danger.   Thus the Platæans escaped through the Spartan lines wearing one shoe only, and in Scotland it used to be the custom for the bridegroom to have one of his shoe-laces untied during the wedding ceremony. (See Major M. Sanderson, *An Examination of the Masonic Ritual*, p. 8).   Here the underlying belief was that by having the shoe unlatched danger or misfortune would be averted.   It seems probable then that the removal of one sh., or the wearing of a sl.p s..d, are alternative forms of the same custom, and that this custom implies first of all that you feel you are in danger and further, that you pledge yourself to carry out some vow if preserved from that danger.

In view of the repeated warnings that the cand. receives of difficulties and dangers which await him, such a precaution is the very first one which would occur to any primitive man conversant with this superstition.

* * *

4. What is the Significance of the C. T.?

This piece of symbolism is very old and world-wide and in Temples in Egypt we see bas-reliefs of cands. being thus led into the Mysteries. Furthermore, on a vase found at Chama, in Mexico, several cands. are depicted going through a ceremony very similar to our 1°. One of them is being taught a s..n well known to every Mason and the other cands., who are waiting their turn, each has a c.. t with a running n...se about his neck.

In India it is the emblem of Yama, the God of Death, with which he snares the souls of men and draws them forth from their bodies, for which reason it is often depicted in the hands of Shiva, who represents the destructive side of the Deity.

Symbolically, therefore, it is an emblem of death and was fastened round the necks of captives to show that they were absolutely at the mercy of their conquerors. It will be remembered that when Calais surrendered to Edward III. six of the leading citizens were compelled to come out and surrender to him, wearing only their shirts and with c. t.s round their necks. Edward III., who was incensed against the City because of its obstinate resistance, only consented to grant it quarters on condition that the Citizens handed over to him six of their leading men to be hung. Six of the chief citizens volunteered to be the victims and thus came out as a willing sacrifice to save the others. To the credit of Edward III. he allowed his wrath to be turned aside by the pleading of Queen Philippa.

Here then we have the most important lesson conveyed by this emblem, for it was in this way that the victims for the burnt sacrifice used to be led round the altar in Jewish and heathen temples.

But the sacrifice God requires is a contrite heart, and seeing that this degree symbolises the spiritual rebirth of the aspirant towards the Light, we may interpret this perambulation with the c. t. round his n..k as indicating that he is prepared to sacrifice his old life so as to gain a new and higher one. Neither can we ignore a secondary, but equally important, meaning. We are captives, bound by the chains of the flesh, and offenders against the law, coming in bondage to sin but seeking to be freed from our bonds by the Word of God.

* * *

5. Should the End of the C. T. be in Front or Behind?

Seeing that the cand. is supposed to be a victim led round a central altar to show that he has been properly prepared to be offered to God, it is clear that the custom which we often see of letting the end of the c. t. hang down aimlessly behind is incorrect. It should, of course, hang in front, as is clearly demonstrated by the phrase towards the end of the ceremony wherein the W.M. warns the cand. that had he attempted to withdraw, etc. Now this statement is quite incorrect if nobody was holding the c. t., and equally incorrect if someone were holding it behind, whereas if the cand. were being led round by the c. t. the instant he tried to back what the Master says would have happened would, indeed, have occurred.

* * *

6. Why is the Cand. H.. w... k.d.?

This procedure is found in every great Initiatory Rite and is intended to remind us that just as we come out of darkness into the light of the physical world, so the same procedure takes place in the intellectual and, finally, in the spiritual worlds. We come into Masonry seeking the light of God's word, that is to say, to comprehend, through the use of symbols, Who and What God really is. Hence, when the h.. w. is removed the first thing we see is the V.S.L., which itself symbolises the Divine Light.

* * *

7. Why does the I.G. use a S. I.?

This is the worn down remnant of those painful tests of courage and self-control which were put to the cands. in the Ancient Mysteries. According to J. Fellows, in "The Mysteries of Freemasonry," p. 147, Pythagoras almost lost his life during his initiation, owing to the severe tests which were applied to him. Even to-day among savages exceedingly painful tests of courage are applied to the youths who are being initiated into manhood. Neither have they entirely died out in Freemasonry, for in the lodges working under the Dutch Constitution, the tests are really quite severe and in the Italian lodges which work in U.S.A. the S.I. is not only applied symbolically, but is driven in at least half an inch.

* * *

8. Why is the Cand. told to step off L. F. first?

In ancient mythology the Preserver is usually depicted as trampling with his left foot on the serpent of evil, or some other monster symbolising sin or ignorance. In ancient Egypt it is in this position that Horus is depicted attacking the great serpent of evil, and Krishna in like manner plants his left foot on a similar evil snake. In Egypt, Horus was the son of Osiris, who came into the world to avenge the murder of his father and overthrow the powers of evil. In India, Krishna is worshipped as an incarnation of God, the Preserver, who is supposed to have descended to earth to help mankind.

The same symbolism prevailed in Christian art, as will be seen from the picture of a Byzantine military saint attacking a lion-like monster, reproduced opposite page 11. Among many races there is a superstition that when entering a shed where food, such as rice, is stored, so as not to hurt the spirit who rules over the rice store, one should enter with the *right* f. first. The right, in short, is the propitious or lucky side, the left, the unlucky. Hence the use of the word sinister, from the Latin word meaning *left*, to imply that something is malign or unpleasant.

On the other hand, when attacking the Spirit of Evil we do desire to hurt him and so, as it were, reverse the superstition and step off left foot first.

So much for old custom and belief, but a medical friend of mine tells me that there is a sound physical reason, and this explains why soldiers are expected to start marching with the left foot. There is always a certain amount of strain thrown upon the heart when starting to advance from a stationary position, and as the left leg is nearer to the heart than the right, less strain is thrown on the heart by moving that first, and thus starting the momentum which carries you forward to the second step.

The implication therefore is that the candidate on entering the lodge symbolically tramples underfoot the powers of evil. In this connection the c.. t. and h. w. represent the trammels of the world. Left f. f. represents trampling on the devil, and the sins of the flesh are symbolically brought under control in the first reg. st., which makes a tau cross, itself the symbol of the phallus and hence, in this connection, of man's physical passions.

*   *   *

9. Why do the Kn...s vary in each of the Degrees?

To symbolise the spiritual progress repre-

A BYZANTINE BRONZE WEIGHT.

sented by each degree. In the first, the candidate has but recently entered the Masonic Order and therefore symbolically has only just been born into the Mystical life. This is portrayed in the three distinct b..s which announce the fact that the lodge is at work in the 1°.

Each b..w represents a part of the triune nature of man, namely, body, soul and spirit. In the E.A. stage these are all of equal importance and are at variance, whereas in the next degree, which symbolises that phase when the work of the E.A. has been accomplished and the physical passions have been brought under control, the soul dominates the body, but as yet the spiritual nature has hardly been aroused. Hence 1/2d.

In the last stage the spirit dominates the soul and the body drops away into insignificance. Hence 2/1d.

* * *

10. Why do the Deacons cross their Wands over the Cand.?

In many countries the triangle is used to represent the maternal, or female, principle, and among the Hindus a man who has lost his caste can be reborn into it by passing through a triangle, which in the case of those desiring Brahmin birth usually has to be made of gold.

Major Sanderson, on p. 12 of "An Examination of the Masonic Ritual," says that the Yaos, a tribe of Nyasaland, have a Rite of Purification, during which they have to pass under a low arch made of two crossed poles, tied together at their intersection, and he adds that the intention is undoubtedly to rid the devotee of clinging evil.

Similar ceremonies occur in Armenia, British Columbia and the Pacific Islands. Furthermore, the original door into the great Pyramid is triangular. This door, which is at a considerable height from the ground, was only discovered in comparatively recent years. That by which tourists usually enter is, of course, not triangular, for it is merely a hole excavated by treasure seekers long after the edifice was erected.

As we are taught that the E.A. degree is the degree of birth, being emblematical of the entry of every man into this, his mortal life, the crossing of the wands, which thus form a triangle, is a very suitable piece of symbolism, representing in plain English the passage of the child through the gateway of birth.

The fact, however, that a triangle instead of the Vesica Piscis is thus employed, suggests a still deeper meaning. Although originally the triangle seems to have represented the female principle, it afterwards came to repre-

sent the triune nature of the Deity, and therefore God and Spirit, and so the crossed wands
not only symbolise birth in general, but a
definitely spiritual birth.

In conclusion it should be remembered that
competent students have long since come to the
conclusion that the Great Pyramid was not an
actual tomb, but a Hall of Initiation wherein
an empty sarcophagus played an important
part. The candidate entered through the
triangular door, symbolically died, passed
through the passages which represented the
Underworld and finally came forth, literally
into the Day.

* * *

**11. What is the meaning of the method by
which the Cand. advances in the 1.?**

This is by three sq....s, which symbolise firstly, uprightness of life and secondly,
abstract justice. Justice is peculiarly an
attribute of God, and the three st...s clearly
refer to His triune nature. There is, however,
a tradition that the letter "G," which in
another degree represents God, should really be
inscribed as a Greek *Gamma*, which is shaped
like a Mason's square. If this be so, we get a
hint at a very profound piece of Kabalism.
Among the Jews God was known by a four letter
name, J H V H, and in order that this should

be made pronounceable the vowels, e, o, a, were inserted when speaking it, making the word *Jehovah*. In Hebrew the names of these letters are Yod, He, Vau, He, the letter He being pronounced Hay. Each of these letters has a gender. Yod is masculine; He is feminine, and Vau, variable. In other words, God the Father, Mother and Child. These first three are symbolised by the three St...s and the fourth letter, the second He, which completes the Sacred Name, is represented by the sq. on the ped. or altar. But, as we have already seen, the letter He is feminine, and its female aspect is emphasied by the position of the sq. and comp..s, which form a lozenge. The latter emblem is a well known substitute for the Vesica Piscis, the symbol of the female, and in heraldry, it is used instead of a shield to contain a woman's coat of arms.

Therefore these st..s conceal a very important truth, namely, that each soul is part of the divine whole and cannot be separated from the God it seeks. Yet notice, there is beyond the candidate more of the Divine. God is veiled so that many do not realise His presence, just as hundreds of candidates make the proper st..s without realising their tremenddous significance, yet it is by this path that the candidate must in reality, as well as in symbolism, draw near to God.

The fact that the fourth square needed to complete the Sacred Name lies on the pedestal is significant, for it warns us that never in the flesh shall we be able to comprehend the nature of God, for no finite man can truly comprehend the Infinite.

* * *

12. What does the Journey round the L. prior to the Ob. Symbolise?

There are many meanings lying hidden in this comparatively simple procedure. Firstly, it represents a victim being brought into the Temple Court to be offered in sacrifice. Secondly, we are told that it is to see that the cand. is prop. pre....d. In reality this means not only that he is prop. pre. but also that he is perfect in all his parts. Hence the regulation in Scotland which definitely forbids the initiation of a maimed, halt or blind man, etc A like regulation still holds in the Roman Catholic Church, where every man desirous of entering the Priesthood must be without serious blemish. In both cases the underlying principle is the same as that which forbade the Jews to offer any animal which was not perfect, "a ram of the first year, without blemish."

This then was the original meaning, but later another and equally important meaning naturally became attached to the ceremony. The fact that the Master says, "brn. in the

North, East, South and West, etc.," shows that the cand. goes round with the sun and this is symbolically the pathway of life, whereas to go the reverse way, West, South, East, North, is to go *widdershins*, which is the path the dead follow through the Underworld.

Such circumambulations play a prominent part alike in religion and magic, and we know also that they formed an essential part of the ritual drama of the Ancient Mysteries. To-day in many countries of the world it is customary to "protect" fields by an annual procession of people carrying torches, which process is supposed to ward off blight and other malign influences.

In the case of our candidate it would seem as if the perambulation symbolises the actual journey into life, whereas the later journey, after he has been entrusted and wherein he is tested, marks the beginning of the actual journey of life itself, which is continued in the second and third degrees.

*   *   *

13. What is meant by the word "Cowan?"

Among the dales in Yorkshire and Lancashire it is usual to enclose a field, not with a hedge, but with a rough wall of stone, built out of pieces of stone which have been gathered up from the field itself. Sometimes these stones are roughly trimmed, but they are not made into true ashlars and are not cemented together. In country places the men who do this work are still called "Cowens," meaning, "rough-wallers," and they are not skilled Masons at all. Hence the word means a man who pretends to be a Mason but knows nothing of the mystery or Craft of Freemasonry.

* * *

14. What is the Origin of the word Tyler?

The word originally meant, "to cover in" and as such was applied to clay sheets which were used to roof a building, and which are still known as tiles. Hence, a man who placed them on the roof was called "a tyler" or one who "covers in."

In a Masonic lodge the duty of the Tyler is to cover in the Lodge and prevent intruders from entering, and the name therefore is derived from the original sense of the word and not from its derivative, "the man who lays tiles."

Certain other derivations of this word have been suggested of which the most interesting is that it comes from the custom which prevailed among the Knights Templar of having two or three watchmen on the roof to give warning if any person were approaching their round churches, in which they held some sort of initiation ceremony, and hence that the name

comes from the French word, *Tailleur*, implying, *one who sits on the tiles*.

It is worth noting that there are traces of a
small tower or turret coming out of the centre of
the roof of some of the old round churches,
which may have served as a kind of sentry box.
For example, before it was restored, the round
Church at Cambridge had such a tower, which,
however, was perpendicular in style, and therefore later than the time of the Templars, but
almost certainly it replaced an old Norman
turret. Unfortunately the restorers swept it
away, but representations of it can be seen in
numerous old prints.

*   *   *

15. What does the word "Hele" mean?

This is derived from an early English word
which still survives in East Anglia and means
"To cover in," having indeed a very similar
significance and use to the word "Tyle."
It is, however, applied to the thatching of the
haystack. The same word is the origin of the
modern word "Hell," which means, "the
Underworld," or "the covered in place," for
according to popular belief, Hell lay under the
earth and consisted of a kind of vast cavern,
hence it was a covered in place.

With regard to the pronunciation of this
word. In the 18th century it and such words

as "conceal" and "reveal" were pronounced like the modern word *Ale*, and there was doubtless a kind of jingle intended. But the pronunciation of words alters in the course of centuries and seeing that the other two words have now changed their pronunciation and this word is really precisely the same as the word "heal," when applied to a wound, there does not seem any particular point in maintaining the old-fashioned pronunciation, which is apt to mislead a candidate into thinking that the word means, "to hail."

*　　*　　*

16. Have the Square and Compasses any further meaning than that which is given in the Ceremony itself?

The position in which they lie on the V.S.L. forms a lozenge, a well known variant of the Vesica Piscis, the symbol of the female principle. This symbol is also repeated in the form of the collars worn by the Officers. Here it is intended to emphasise the female or preservative side of the Deity, without which we could not exist for a single day or hope to be preserved from the powers of darkness, and no matter how the position of the points of the c...s may vary in each degree the shape of the lozenge is always maintained.

*　　*　　*

17. In some Lodges I have visited in the North of England, instead of the V.S.L. being placed on the Master's Ped. it rests on a smaller ped. or altar half way between the Master's Ped. and the centre of the room, can you explain the variation?

There is little doubt that historically the separate altar is the older method and it has much to recommend it. It is hardly dignified or fitting that the three great Lights in Masonry should, as now often happens, serve as a repository for the Master's agenda.

Moreover, the central, cubicle altar is very ancient. Thus we find such an altar in what is known as *The Hall of the Axe* at Knossos, in Crete, circa 2,000 B.C. This chamber has stone benches along the sides of the walls and at the end opposite the door is an elaborate stone seat, obviously intended for the Master of the Mysteries which were once worked in this ancient lodge room.

It should be noted that there are many minor variations in the working of our Ceremonies in different parts of the country, most of which are valuable because they throw interesting side-lights on the meaning of the various degrees.

* * *

18. Is there any hidden significance in the fact that the Cand. is placed in the N.E. Corner?

Yes, the first point being that in ancient days it was customary to bury a victim under the foundation stone and numerous examples of this custom have been found, particularly in Palestine, where it is usually an unfortunate babe whose skeleton is revealed when excavators are exploring the foundations of some ancient edifice.

Even as late as the end of the 16th century the Turks buried a Christian Martyr in a hole, which they filled with cement and made the foundation stone of one of their forts at Algiers. His fate was well known and when the French took that town in the 19th century they actually broke open the block of cement and found some of the bones and the hollow cast made by his body. They ran plaster into it and this somewhat gruesome relic is now in their museum at Algiers, while the bones of the martyr, who has been duly canonised under the name of St. Geronamus are now one of the most precious relics in the Cathedral at that City.

Even to-day in England a last, faint memory of this ancient custom survives, in that coins bearing the effigy of a man, i.e., the King, are placed under the foundation stones of important buildings. Thus the candidate is placed at the North East corner symbolically to represent a Foundation Sacrifice.

The original idea underlying such foundation sacrifices was the belief that the soul of the victim would enter into the building and give it life, so that the stones would be welded together, as is the case in a living organism, such as a tree. In other words, the sacrifice was made in order that the building might stand firm for ever. We have already seen that the candidate is led in like a victim prepared for sacrifice, the pen. represents the method of sacrifice adopted, and this last incident explains the object of the sacrifice, namely that symbolically each candidate dedicates his life to the task of making the whole Masonic edifice stand firm for ever.

* * *

19. Why is the Foundation Stone laid in the North East Corner?

This was for a very practical reason, namely, so that the workmen could lay the course with the sun and thus obtain a maximum amount of light. Starting at six in the morning, they would, as it were, follow the sun to eventide.

Symbolically it refers to the journey of the soul, which begins in the North and enters mortal life at birth in the East, and so proceeds via the South to the West, which denotes death.

* * *

20. Why is the Cand. told to stand in such a Peculiar Manner when placed in the North East?

The position in which the cand. stands is not only a square, emblematical of rectitude and of God, but at the particular point named the feet constitute an angle clamp, which binds together the life which has been—in the North, which represents pre-natal experience—and the new life which is just beginning, in the East, which symbolises mortal life.

In spiritual things the North is the place of darkness, the condition we are in before we turn towards the light. It should be noted that such angle clamps, which are by no means uncommon in old buildings, give rigidity and strength to the corners and so assure stability.

*   *   *

21. What do the Three Principal Officers Symbolise?

These officers symbolise the triune nature of God and man and according as we view them from one or other of these angles, our explanation of each varies. Taking the Divine Triad first, they represent the Creative, Preservative, and Annihilative or Transformative sides of the Deity, and they link up with the sun in its three great phases.

Thus the W.M. represents the rising sun at

Dawn, and therefore God, the Creator. It is he who calls the lodge into being out of nothingness, just as God created the world out of chaos. In India this aspect of God is called by the name of Brahma, and by us, T.G.A.O.T.U. It will be noticed that the Master opens the lodge and sits in the East, the place of light, but he does not close it, a significant fact, that work being reserved for another officer, who symbolises the destructive side of the Deity.

The J.W. represents the sun at its meridian, and in the Divine aspect, God the Preserver, Whom the Hindus call Vishnu, and we, the G.G.O.T.U. Vishnu is associated with the element of water and of corn, and his caste mark is a perpendicular, straight line, in reference to the rain which falls from Heaven. This symbol is remembered in our lodges by the plumb rule. In the Masonic allegory he represents H.A.B. In all the great religions of the world we find an aspect of God called the Preserver, Who becomes incarnate and suffers death for the sake of man, as, for example, Krishna, in India, or Osiris in Egypt, a fact which should be correlated with the story of H.A.B.

The S.W. represents the Setting Sun, and hence the Destructive or Transformative side of the Deity. Among the Hindus this aspect is named Shiva, and among us, The Most High. It is the S.W. who closes the lodge, and his level reminds us of the caste mark of Shiva, which is a horizontal line. Like Shiva, he is also to some extent identified with the Moon.

Turning to the human aspect, the W.M. represents the Divine Spark, the Spirit in every man, and the S.W., the Soul, which alone is in a position to enable the Spirit to raise the body towards divine things, for without the medium of the Soul the Spirit would be unable to influence the body at all. That is why the S.W., symbolising the soul, invests the cand., and not the W.M.. The J.W., of course, represents the Body, the only one of the three which can perish at the hands of traitors; that is why it is the duty of the J.W. to be the nominal steward of the lodge and call the brethren from labour to refreshment. He symbolises physical life.

*   *   *

CHAPTER II.

THE FELLOW CRAFT.

22. What is the Origin of the T.B.s?

In the 18th century candidates were not rushed from one degree to another after learning parrot-wise merely a few phrases. On the contrary, a considerable time elapsed, and at the intervening meetings what were known as *The Lectures*, were delivered. Apparently these were given after the banquet and were illustrated and memorised by means of drawings made in sand on the floor of the room. My readers will recollect that in the 18th century, and indeed well into the 19th century, it was customary to strew sand on the stone floor of an inn and it would therefore be quite easy to draw various designs on this sand with a staff.

In the course of years the use of sand was abandoned in favour of chalk and the figures and designs were drawn on the floor in that medium, being subsequently washed away by the initiate, for we get references in the old Minutes to the fact that the candidate had to use the mop and pail to wipe out the T.B..

When it became customary to cover the lodge floor with an elaborate carpet both these primitive expedients became impossible and a board placed on tressels took the place of a drawing on the floor. Finally, towards the end of the 18th or beginning of the 19th century, a design painted on canvas replaced the tressel board.

At first these designs were more or less extemporised on the spur of the moment but later a traditional series of pictures established themselves and these are what we have to-day. So far as the Lectures are concerned, they consisted of a number of questions put by the Master to another officer, usually the S.W. What we now call the Lecture on the T.B. was a summary of these questions given to the candidate to enable him to memorise the chief incidents, and help him to answer correctly when he was questioned on being passed to the next degree.

*   *   *

23. At High Noon. Why this Paradox?

In Operative days lodges were held at mid-day and probably on a Saturday, after the workmen had received their wages. The Speculatives, for their own convenience, changed the time to the evening, and this being so brethren may well wonder why this untrue statement is still left in the ritual. The reason is symbolical. At mid-day the sun is at its full strength and so this is the most suitable time for a Solar

Cult to hold its meetings. Furthermore, the J.W., we are told, represents the sun at its meridian and this officer represents the body. Therefore this sentence implies that the meetings are held when the body is at its full strength and in possession of all its faculties.

On the other hand, we find that the great Masonic tragedy occurred at High Noon and those brethren who look for a Christian interpretation underlying our ceremonies will not overlook the fact that Christ was hung on the cross at 12, Noon.

In other words, the lodge symbolically re-enacts the ancient drama at the exact time when it was supposed to have occurred.

In France, indeed, the point is further emphasised by a question which occurs at the Opening of the Lodge, when the W.M. asks the S.W., "What time is it?" and the latter replies, "Midi."

* * *

24. What are the Perfect Points of my Entry?

The answer to this is found in the Lectures, of which the questions put to the Cand. are of course really a summary. In these Lectures the answer is "Of, at and on," meaning, "Of my own free will and accord; at the door of the lodge; on the p. of a S.I."

* * *

25. Why are P.W.s Used?

In olden days it was believed that by certain ceremonies it was possible for a group of men to raise themselves to a higher key, and that such a body all concentrating on a particular subject generated a peculiar, subtle, but powerful force which, although it has not been accurately defined by science, is loosely called "Magnetic."

In the old days of phenomenal magic, certain words when uttered in the correct tone were believed to be in consonance with this power, like a tuning fork is to a violin.

Now while the cand. is out of the room, being prepared, the lodge is raised from the first to the second degree, and therefore in order that the cand. may be quickly raised to the same power as the lodge a P.W. is given to him. Such P.W.s were used in all the great Mysteries and they must not be confounded with the w. of the degree.

*   *   *

26. If a P.W. is necessary in the 2° why was the Cand. not given one at his Initiation?

As a matter of fact in Ireland and in most parts of Scotland he is given one, and although the cand. is not taught one in the English working, and is not even told that he receives one, it is actually spoken for him, and that no

less than four times. The Tyler gives it to the
I.G. and the latter gives it to the W.M., both
these occasions being on the entry of the Cand.
into the Lodge.   Later the D. gives it to the
J.W. and the S.W..   The word is "the t.o.
good r...t."   Sometimes "Free and of g. r."
is substituted.

Now in Ireland one of the first tests applied
to a stranger claiming to be a Mason is to ask
him for the P.W. leading to the 1°, and many
an English brother has found himself in serious
difficulties because he did not know that these
words actually constitute the P.W..

* * *

27. What is the Inner Meaning of the Word Sh.?

In Freemasonry the interpretations of the
various w..s given in the ceremony are nearly
always incorrect; possibly this is deliberate.
In the case of this word, the meaning is not p.,
but literally, "an ear of corn" or alternatively,
"a fall of water," hence the manner in which
it is depicted on the T.B. of a F.C. Lodge.

It is interesting to note that in the Eleusinian
Mysteries one of the most dramatic points in
the ceremony was when an ear of corn was
shown to the initiate, and at the same time an
officer emptied an ewer of water on to the
ground.   Whereupon the whole of the onlookers
cried to the great earth Mother, "Conceive".

Symbolically, however, the translation given "P." conveys a very important lesson. Corn and water constitute the barest necessities, without which human life cannot be sustained, yet they are here declared to be synonymous with p...y. This implies that to the spiritu-ally-minded man a simple diet, the mere necessities of life, are quite sufficient, whereas wealth, which brings with it luxury, destroys the soul, a lesson hinted at in the P.W. lead-ing from the 2° to the 3° when considered in conjunction with the dramatic indicent which happens soon afterwards.

* * *

28. Why in this Degree is the R. instead of the L. Kn. made B.?

In the former degree it was pointed out that the l. side has always been associated with the feminine, probably because it is the weaker, and so synonymous with the so-called weaker sex. In the first degree we are babies, just born, and during infancy the child is almost entirely under the control of the women of the household. This is particularly the case in Eastern countries, where up to the age of seven the small boy has the free run of the harem and is looked after almost entirely by the women. But the second degree symbolises life and edu-cation, in short, adolescence and manhood.

In the East, after the age of seven the boy ceases to have the run of the harem and comes under the direct control of his father and other male relatives. He is instructed in manly exercises and goes to some school, perhaps one attached to a Mosque, where he is taught by a man.

In the West, although the same process is probably delayed for a few years, in like manner the boy passes from the control of women to school and college.

Hence it is quite natural that in this degree, which emphasises adolescence and manhood, and conveys to us the lesson that all life is educational, the right, or masculine, side should be stressed.

*   *   *

29. What is the Inner Significance of the Square?

We have previously pointed out that the square is the same shape as the Greek letter "Gamma," which many competent students believe was the form of the letter "G" usually depicted in our lodges in ancient days to represent T.G.G.O.T.U., but apart from this the square seems to have been a sacred emblem from the very earliest times.

In Babylon we find it as the symbol of Nabu, the Architect god of the Babylonians, who was supposed to have created the world. His square, unlike our square and that used by the Egyptians, was the gallows square, with the end of the two arms joined by a third line. It thus formed a right-angle triangle having one long, one medium and one short side.

It is in Egypt, however, that we get the closest analogy to our symbolic use of the square. With these people it was the emblem of justice, for which reason when the Gods are depicted sitting in judgment on the dead they are always shown seated on squares, and it should be noted that when the Gods are not seated in judgment the square does not appear on their chairs or thrones.

A very good example of this occurs in the papyrus of Ani in the scene depicting the weighing of Ani, where the twelve assessors all have squares depicted on their thrones. Since no one could pass through this trial successfully unless he proved that he had lived a good moral life, the square naturally became the emblem as well as the test of moral rectitude.

The square is also sacred in China, where the legendary founder of the Chinese State, Fu Hsi, always bears as his emblem the gallows square, while his wife holds a pair of compasses. The earliest extant records of this legendary ancestor are bas-reliefs of the Han Dynasty, circa 100 B.C.

Its peculiar association with the second degree is no doubt to emphasise the fact that during mortal life a man must learn rectitude of conduct and treat with justice his fellow men, for only of such can it be truly said "to the just and upright man, death hath no terrors."

*   *   *

32.   Why is the Cand. told to Advance to-wards the Ped. in the 1° and towards the East in the 2°?

In the first he was h.. w.. and therefore quite unable to tell in which direction the East lay, but in the 2° not only can he see, but his previous experience tells him the point in the compass where he will take his ob.

Symbolically this teaches us that in the 1° he had no clear idea where to seek for the light, he was merely groping blindly, although led by a friendly hand.   But, having in the previous degree learnt that the true light comes from the East, he understands perfectly why he is instructed to advance in that direction. It is worth mentioning that in the Lectures one of the first questions put to the E.A. is to ask whence he comes and whither he is going, to which he answers that he comes from the W. and is going to the E. in search of a Master, from whom he hopes to obtain instruction. Having theoretically given this answer in the

course of the training preparatory to his taking
the 2°, it is but natural that he should be told
to continue his journey towards the East. In-
cidentally these answers should be compared
with the somewhat similar questions in the
Opening of the 3°, noting, however, the
important difference.

* * *

**31. How is it that the W..d..g St..c..e
is said to have 3, 5, 7 or more steps?**

This is clearly an allegory, the object disguised under this name being each individual
man. Man consists of the three who rule,
namely, the Body, Soul and Spirit, corresponding with H.A.B., Hiram the King, and Solomon, or, from another standpoint, the Master
and his two Wardens.

The number 5 refers to the five senses, which
are often used to symbolise man himself. But
every physical man has both a soul and a spirit,
and each of the latter are believed to have a
special faculty not possessed by the body and
therefore superimposed on the five physical
senses. The soul has what are called the
psychic senses, such as second sight, and the
Spirit has mystical and inspirational powers.
It was these powers which enabled the prophets
to speak by Divine inspiration.

Although while on earth the ordinary man

only functions through his five physical senses, those who are approaching perfection, such as the great religious teachers and Masters, function through all seven. Furthermore, in connection with this number seven as symbolising man it is as well to remember that the ancient Egyptians sub-divided man into seven parts, considering that there were five sub-sections of the Soul; in addition to the Body and the Divine Spark. It is also partly due to this tradition inherited from ancient Egypt that the number seven has so emphatically been retained in our rituals, but it should be noted the compilers thereof were careful to cover themselves by saying "seven or more," indicating that it is quite possible that later scientists may be able to sub-divide man even more minutely than the ancient Egyptians.

It may be as well to add, however, that the reference to the five noble orders of architecture is clearly an 18th century innovation, for our ancient brethren in the Middle Ages had entirely forgotten these artificial sub-divisions of classical architecture. But for all that they key into the allegory, namely, that every man is engaged in building a Temple for the Most High, a Temple of the Holy Ghost, wherein all his five senses will find their appropriate stations.

*   *   *

32. Why is it a *W..d..g* St...c..e?

This is rather an important point, for it will be noted that when asecnding you advance neither to the East nor to the West, but still revolve around the centre, a fact that should be correlated with the p. within the c. which appears upon the T.B. of the 1°. As usually depicted in our lodges, the w..d..g st...c..e is so badly drawn that if it were really built so it would instantly collapse. What is really intended is one of the spiral staircases such as one gets in a Mediæval Castle or Church tower.

To an Eastern brother this will certainly recall the ladder of re-incarnation, by the gradual ascent of which the soul in time returns to God, travelling upwards in a circle. To Westerners, as previously stated, it is our body, subdued, brought under control and dedicated to the glory of God.

* * *

33. What then is the Middle Ch.?

It is that secret recess within the soul where lies hidden the Divine Spark. Our wages are knowledge of God. An experience which each must discover for himself and in himself, as every Mystic has taught, and it is only when we have trampled under foot and brought under control the sins of the senses, etc., that we

master his five senses, but still it is only by
permission, or by the way, of his soul that he
can become cognisant of the Divine Spark
hidden within his own being and the nature of
God with whom it is in Union.

*   *   *

36.   What do the two Pillars shown on the T.B. symbolise?

Throughout the world pillars have from the
most primitive times been regarded as phalli,
emblems of the male generative principle, and
the translation of the name of the junior pillar
definitely implies this phallic significance.
Symbolically therefore it stands for the creative
power in man and God.   From its presence we
are supposed to learn the importance of spiritual creation, of which the building of the
Temple of God is another allegory.

The Jews, despite the teaching of the prophets,
often lapsed into worship of similar pillars,
which are called *Massebah*, and these were set
in a socket.   Sometimes they were made of
wood and then they were called *Asherah*.
Jeremiah denounces their backsliding (Chapter
II v. 27) "Saying to a stock Thou art my Father
(a wooden pillar) and to a stone, Thou hast
begotten me."

In Egypt two pillars *tat* and *tattu* were annually set up with a number of Rites, and a simi-

A 13th CENTURY MOSAIC FROM TORCELLO, CONTAINING A SUBTLE REFERENCE TO THE TAŪ CROSS.

lar pair were fabled to stand at the entrance to Amenta, the Underworld. Through these the dead passed on their way to the Realm of Osiris.

In ancient Egyptian the word *Tat* means *Strength*, and *Tattu, to establish firmly*. Lucian tells us that two great bronze phalli stood in front of the temple of Heirapolis in Syria, and in ancient Babylonia similar pillars are depicted on a seal between which the Sun God is shown rising from the Underworld.

Thus a pair of pillars not only symbolises Creation but also the Gateway of Birth.

* * *

37. Why is the F.C. told that he is PER-MITTED to extend his Researches?

Only a few minutes before the candidate has been told that he is *expected* to do this, and in consequence many brethren have rushed to the conclusion that the word is a mis-print for expected. If this were so the two passages would constitute a needless duplication, and the second would be better expunged. As a matter of fact, however, there is not the slightest doubt that the word permitted is old and intentionally inserted here, constituting a valuable piece of evidence of the antiquity of our ceremonies.

In the Ancient Mysteries it was believed that

the Masters of the Higher Grades possessed certain important secrets of nature or, in plain English, had certain occult powers, such as that of hypnotising and of healing, and consequently of the reverse to healing. Even to-day in India the higher class of Yogi claims to possess these same powers, for which very reason the Masters of this Science will not advance their disciples to these higher grades until they have had them under observation for many years and have satisfied themselves that they are men of the highest moral truth and virtue, or as it might be put, only when they have made themselves acquainted with the principles of moral truth and justice are they permitted to extend their researches into the hidden mysteries of occult science.

Even if we put aside occult powers we shall be compelled to admit that the promiscuous disclosure to all and sundry of the secrets of nature discovered by science has not been an unmixed blessing to man. For example, the invention of poison gas if persisted in, brought to the highest efficiency possible, and combined with the modern aeroplane, may one day completely destroy its discoverers and with them civilisation itself. In other words, men are probing into the mysteries of nature and science before they have acquired that exaltation of moral character which renders their knowledge of benefit to themselves and humanity.

CHAPTER III.

THE SUBLIME DEGREE.

38. What Does T.C. Mean?

Major Sanderson in his "Examination of the Masonic Ritual" says that in Hebrew this word means merely "a Blacksmith," although another word, similarly pronounced, means, "acquisition": hence a professional name has by the translator been mistaken for that of an actual person. In short, the cand. states that he is a worker in me..ls. It will be remembered that in the Bible H.A.B. is not described as a Mason but as a worker in metals, a fact that is stressed in the second degree by the statement in the T.B. that it was he who cast the two brazen pillars, etc.. Thus, following this line of interpretation, we perceive that the cand. really represents H.A.B. when he enters the lodge, although under a disguised title, long before he is told the legend of that great man.

Symbolically the interpretation as to wealth conveys a valuable lesson. The F.C. is one who finds the simple necessities of life, such as corn and water, sufficient for his requirements, but the acquisition of wealth (T. C.) brings

death to the soul and prevents its upward progress.

S. L. Knapp, in "The Secret Discipline,"
says, "By a singular *plausus linguae* the moderns
have substituted T. C. in the 3° for *Tymboxein*
—to be entombed." I am unable to say
whether Knapp is justified in this statement,
but it is quite probable that this word, and
indeed all the words, are comparatively modern
substitutes, culled from the Bible to replace
ancient words of power whose form had become
corrupt by oral transmission and whose meaning was therefore unintelligible. This Greek
word would be peculiarly suitable for a p. w.
leading to the sublime degree.

Mediæval magical ceremonies are full of corrupt Greek works, indescriminately mingled
with equally corrupt Hebrew and Arabic ones,
and even the Latin rituals of the Western
Church still retain a few Greek words such as
Kyrie eleison. There is therefore nothing
improbable in the suggestion that this Greek
word was the original from which T.C. evolved.
We know that in the 18th century large pieces
of Biblical history were imported wholesale into
our ritual, and so it is quite probable that an
unintelligible word, already so corrupt as not
even to be recognisable as Greek, should be
amended into a well-known Biblical character.

*   *   *

39. In the Opening Ceremony the W.M. promises to assist the Brethren to seek for what is L..t, but apparently he immedi-ately forgets all about it and proceeds to Initiate the Cand. Can you explain this?

In reality the ceremony of rais. describes the journey from the East to the West and implies that the l. s...ts can only be rediscovered beyond the grave. The l. s..ts are the com-prehension of the nature of God and the method of our return to Him, and seeing that the finite cannot comprehend the infinite the Master helps us to find those l. s..ts by telling us exactly where they are, namely, beyond the grave, for it is only by death that we shall learn alike of the nature of God and of eternal life.

* * *

40. What is that which was Lost?

Comprehension of the nature of God, a realis-ation of the fact that there is a Divine Spark within us which is ever linked in some mysteri-ous way with the Divine Being, and the method of our return to God, from Whom we came, which latter is by the Path of Self-sacrifice and Death.

* * *

41. What is meant by the P. within the C.?

The circle is the emblem of eternity and there-

fore of spirit, and the p. at the centre symbolises
consciousness. In Egypt this emblem symbolised Ra, the King of all the Gods. In astrology
it is used to represent the Sun, whose importance
in Masonry we have already seen, but it is in
India that we undoubtedly obtain its original
significance. There it is used to represent
Paramatma, the Supreme Being, the One True
God, Who lies behind all the gods, and from
Whom both Gods and men, and even inanimate
things, are but emanations, existing only because they have closed within their matter a
tiny spark of Paramatma. Naturally, therefore,
at the c. of the c. rests all knowledge and so
there we shall find the l.. s...ts.

Moreover, if we substitute for the phrase p.
within the c., the word "God," we shall find
that we say that the s...ts are with God. This
fact is important, for the phrase "with the c."
does not mean, by means of the centre, which
would make no sense, but that in the words of
St. John "The Word is with God," a sentence
used at the Closing of every Lodge working
under the Scotch Constitution.

Seeing, however, that man is a microcosm of
God, the p. with the c. also has a reference to
each individual. The p. is the small fragment
of conscious personality which lies at the c. of
a vast, sub-conscious self, and hidden in or
at this centre is the Divine Spark, which links

us with the Source of our being, so that from that c. no M.M. can ever err.

*   *   *

42. Why over an Open Gr.?

This is a very ancient custom and is connected with the belief that if a woman steps over a g. wherein lies a dead body the soul of the deceased will enter into her womb and be reborn. Symbolically, however, it conveys the valuable lesson that we can only reach the s...s of a M.M., i.e., knowledge of the Infinite and Supreme Being, by passing through the g..

*   *   *

43. Why are there Seven St...s?

Three represents God, because of His triune nature, and four was supposed to symbolise matter, the earth, and finally our physical bodies, because of the four elements of which each of the latter is supposed to be composed. Three and four make the perfect number, seven, so called because it represents all things in Heaven and Earth, God and Man. Hence seven steps mean that we dedicate the whole of our nature—body, soul and spirit—and in the process will raise that nature to Union with God.

*   *   *

44. Why are the St...s in the form of a Cr...s?

The manner of advancing forms the Cross of

an angel, an archangel, a demi-god and so forth, until, as the most exalted of all spirits, he finally, in the fifteenth stage, reaches at-one-ment, or union, with the Supreme Being.

It will be remembered that the ladder on the T.B. in the 1° is usually, and should always be, depicted with fifteen rungs to it.   Among the Jews fifteen was the sum of the numerical equivalents of the Hebrew letters which from the word Jah, meaning God.

*   *   *

48.   What do the three Vil...ns represent?

According to one interpretation they represent the three Winter months which oppress the Sun, the cand. symbolically representing that luminary and suffering with him, just as in ancient Egypt the soul of the dead was supposed to accompany the Sun on its journey through the Underworld.

From the symbolical standpoint they represent the lust of the flesh, the lust of the eye and the pride of life.   In other words, the sins of the flesh, the sins of the soul—such as covetousness—and spiritual pride, which is the most fatal of all.

Those who consider that there is a Christian interpretation permissible even in the Craft, will perceive in these three scoundrels Herod, Caiphas and Pontius Pilate.

*   *   *

49. What is the meaning of H.A.B.?

In Hebrew this name means quite a number of things. *Ab* means "His father," and Hiram means, "exaltation of Life," "liberty or whiteness," "he that destroys." It is moreover possible that the second word is a corruption of *Abib*, a Hebrew word signifiying "Ears of corn," or "green fruits." As in all the Ancient Mysteries the allegory dramatised represented an ear of corn which was planted in the ground, i.e., slain and buried, and subsequently rose again in the form of a bountiful harvest, this possible explanation must not be overlooked. On the other hand, taking the reading as the one which is given, we find that the meaning of the name is, "The father of the exaltation of Life," or, "the father of he who destroys."

The exaltation of life reminds us of the legend that Shiva, the Hindu form of God the Destroyer, on a certain day increased his stature until he overtopped the universe. As a result all the gods, including Brahma and Vishnu, were obliged to acknowledge him as being supreme. He therefore gathered unto himself the beginning and the end of all things, Alpha and Omega, and henceforth both death and birth alike were in his hands.

With regard to liberty, to the pious Hindu, Shiva by death grants liberty from the toils and anguish of this world and sets the soul saying that it was the spirit of Polydorus who was speaking. The spirit then went on to relate that he had been murdered secretly by the King of Thrace and hidden in this spot. Numerous examples could be quoted, such as that in the story of the Two Brothers, wherein the soul of one of the brothers entered into an acacia tree, a tree, of course, sacred to Osiris. I have little doubt that in the earlier form of our legend the sprig of acacia also spoke, thereby revealing what was hidden and informing the seekers of the sad fate of the Master, it being indeed his own soul speaking from the acacia bush. Such a story seeming too far-fetched for Anderson and his matter of fact friends, they doubtless edited this part of the story, giving a more practical explanation of this emblem.

The appropriateness of the acacia as an emblem of the resurrection lies in the fact that it grows in sandy, desert soil in North Africa, stands drought well, and produces a mass of green foliage and fragrant yellow blossoms, rather similar to Mimosa. It also has enormous thorns, and tradition avers that it was with a wreath of these acacia thorns that Christ was crowned by the soldiers of Pilate. As already indicated, it plays a large part in the legend of Osiris and a tree of it was supposed to grow at the entrance to the Underworld

*   *   *

52. Why is it called the L..n's Gr.?

Of recent years there has grown up a tendency to drop the use of this name for the gr. of an M.M.. This is a thousand pities, for it is a very ancient landmark and is traceable back to Palestine and Egypt. In the latter country the Supreme God, whether spoken of as Ra or Osiris, is constantly addressed as "The God in the Lion Form." Major Sanderson points out that in such cases the prayer is that the soul of the departed may be permitted to come forth in the East, rising with the Sun from the darkness of the grave. He adds that the lion not only personified strength and power but is almost exclusively associated with the regeneration of the sun, and hence with the resurrection. It is for this reason that Osiris is called, *The Lion of Yesterday*, and Ra, *The Lion of Tomorrow*, and that the former's bier is always represented as having the head and legs of a lion. Naturally, therefore, the beds or biers found in the tombs of Tut-ankh-amen are similarly lion-like in form. It is even possible that the reason the Sign Leo is given that designation is that it is the first Sign of the Zodiac entered by the Sun after the Solstice. Hence the name, l. gr. as specifying the manner by which the cand. is r....d is very important and it should be noted that Albert Pike, the great American Masonic writer, in his "Morals and Dogma" shows a representation, stated to be from an Egyptian picture, wherein a Lion is depicted seizing by the wrist a man who is apparently lying dead in front of an altar. Behind the altar stands a figure whose left arm is elevated in the form of a square, and it seems clear that the lion is in the act of raising the dead man.

Among the Jews the Lion was a symbol of royalty. The King of Judah was called the Lion of the tribe of Judah, and among later writers the term became a symbol for the promised Messiah.

It was for this reason that the Comacine Masons, who carried on the Masonic tradition after the collapse of the Roman Empire, adopted it as their emblem to such an extent that with the endless knot it has become almost a hall-mark of their work. A very striking example occurs on the West front of the Cathedral at Arles, which is 12th century work, but numerous other examples might be quoted.

* * *

53. What is meant by, That Bright Morning Star?

According to Major Sanderson this is a figurative allusion to Sirius or Sothis, the Dog Star, which by its rising at dawn gave warning of the approaching inundation of the Nile in Egypt. It was only this inundation which saved Egypt from becoming a desert like the surrounding country, and hence it truly betokened peace and salvation to the whole of Egypt.

It was not only in Egypt, however, that a certain bright Morning Star was so significant, for in Syria and Palestine, the Rising of Venus as the Bright Morning Star which heralds the Dawn played an important part in the Rites of Adonis. When Venus appeared in the East at Dawn Adonis was fabled to ascend to Heaven, and this usually occurred about the Spring Equinox. In ancient Britain it was when Sirius appeared in a certain position, that is, in a line with the great sacrificial stone at Stonehenge, that the greatest human sacrifices were offered, and this also was at the Spring Equinox.

The crescent moon with the star between the horns was usually depicted on the head of Astarte in Syria, of Ishtar in Babylonia and of Isis in Egypt, and this same crescent and star became associated with the Virgin Mary and Christianity and is, of course, the badge of Islam.

We thus see that the Star is a very ancient symbol, closely associated with death and resurrection, or alternatively with birth and re-birth, in all the Ancient Mysteries. We must not forget, however, that from the 5th to the 18th century Masonry was unquestionably Christian: Anderson indeed admits it, and the ancient charges prove it beyond doubt. Hence we are perfectly justified in considering that this emblem was retained right through the Middle Ages because it was regarded as referring to the Star which led the Wise Men to Bethlehem and pointed out the birth of the Saviour of the World, He Who should ultimmately triumph over death by rising from the grave.

*   *   *

54. What does the Skirrit Represent?

The skirrit in a somewhat humbler shape is still used by gardeners to assist them in planting seeds in a straight line, and of course can be used by Masons to mark the straight lines along which the foundations for a building are to be built. It is also used for keeping the walls straight as they rise from the foundation. Undoubtedly, however, the emblem was adopted because of its similarity to the Caduceus of Mercury, although as far back as the time of the Roman Collegia it was clearly recognised as a symbol of Freemasonry.

In the ruins of the Roman College of Architects at Pompeii is a corner stone whereon are engraved the principal working tools of a Mason: they include a heavy maul, a pair of compasses, a gavel and chisel, a combined square, level and plumb rule, and above all, a skirrit. The full significance of this stone is shown in the answer to Question 82, but the presence of the skirrit so far back historically is significant.

The skirrit, however, has more than a superficial resemblance to the Caduceus of Mercury and Sir John Coburn has suggested that it was substituted for this "heathen emblem." I agree with his views, for it is clear that at the beginning of the 19th century a deliberate attempt was made to eliminate this emblem from our ceremonies. In the 18th century the jewel of the Deacons was not a dove but a figure of Mercury, bearing the Caduceus. A number of these old jewels are in the museum at Grand Lodge and there are still a few old lodges which continue to use them. Members of the Mark degree will recollect that the Caduceus, instead of the dove, appears on the jewel of the deacons.

Mercury was the Messenger of the Gods but, still more important, he was supposed to conduct the souls through the Underworld to the Elysian Fields and before his Caduceus the powers of evil fled. In Mediæval eschatology it is Christ who leads the souls on a similar journey, uplifting in His Hand the Cross of Salvation, which has replaced the heathen emblem. I have little doubt therefore that the skirrit, being an instrument which shows the Operative Mason where his footings should run, was in ancient times regarded as the emblem of Caduceus, and even to-day has been permitted to survive because to those who look beneath the surface it symbolises the journey beyond the grave, and he who leads the candidate thereon.

* * *

55. Why is the Apron made of Lamb's Skin?

The lamb was the Jewish victim of sacrifice and it is doubtless for this reason that our aprons are always made of lamb's skin, although by the Mediæval period the lamb had become an emblem of innocence.

The use of leather, much less of sheep-skin, for our aprons is in curious contradiction with the custom of the Egyptians, who regarded the hides of animals as unclean. Indeed, they laid it down that the corpses of criminals who had been executed were to be wrapt in sheep-skins and flung into the city moat, it being believed that in consequence of the defiling nature of the sheep-skin their souls would fail to pass the guardians of the Egyptian Underworld.

Although no doubt there is a symbolic meaning in the use of lamb's skin, we must not forget that the Operative Masons wore aprons for a purely utilitarian reason, and these were made of hide, which was more durable than any woven material. That a tough material like this was essential is obvious when we remember that a mason is constantly handling pieces of stone. These Mediæval aprons, however, bore very little resemblance to our modern ornate badges. They consisted of the hide of a sheep or lamb, of which most of the forelegs and the tail had been removed. The head formed the bib and the rest of the skin covered the whole of the body, coming down at least to the knees.

This type of apron continued in use even in Speculative Masonry as late as the time of the artist Hogarth, who has left us a print of a couple of Masons coming back from lodge and wearing just such a primitive apron as I have described.

Every brother who receives an apron, and more especially the E.A., should bear in mind that not only is it the badge of innocence and of sacrifice but that actually the life of the original owner has to be sacrificed, an innocent lamb slain, before a Mason's apron can be made.

*   *   *

56.   Why has it a flap and three rosettes?

The three rosettes symbolise the rose, itself a substitute for the vesica piscis—the symbol for the female—and with the colour, light blue, these imply that the Master Mason's duty is to serve rather than to command. Light blue, the colour of Heaven, is also the colour of Isis and the Virgin Mary, and hence is symbolical of the feminine, whereas dark blue is symbolical of the masculine.

It will be noticed that the three rosettes are arranged so as to form a triangle whose point is upward, interpenetrating the triangle formed by the flap of the apron. The two triangles only interpenetrate half way, thus differing from the double triangle seen on the R.A. jewel.

The lower triangle, with its point upwards, is the emblem of fire and so of the Divine Spark. It also symbolises Shiva, the Destroyer. The triangle made by the flap of the apron has its point downward and symbolises the triangle of water. It therefore represents the soul, which is regarded as feminine and as unstable as water. The two triangles are within the square and so symbolise the complex nature of man, consisting of body, soul and spirit.

Viewed from another standpoint, the triangle represents spirit and the square, matter. In the first degree the flap or triangle should point upwards towards the chin, a piece of symbolism which should be, but is not always, observed in every lodge. It implies that the spirit has not yet really entered matter, (a hint of the pre-natal stage) or at any rate has acquired no control over the body, which is certainly true of the newborn infant. In the second degree the spirit has entered and has obtained at least some control over its material envelope. In the 3rd degree the appearance of the upward pointing triangle warns us that death is at hand, for it is the emblem of the Destroyer which penetrates even into the triangle of spirit.

*   *   *

57. Why is the Apron fastened with a Serpent?

From the foregoing answers it will be clear that our aprons are comparatively modern and so is their symbolism, and this is particularly true of the present arrangement with which the apron is fastened, which consists of a piece of webbing with a hook and eye attachment. Before the 19th century aprons were fastened by means of strings, and to this day the aprons used by those Grand Lodge officers who have duties to perform in Grand Lodge, as distinct from those who receive Past Grand rank, still have strings instead of webbing and the snake clasp. I feel, however, that it was not accident which led to the adoption of the snake for this purpose. It must be realised that there are two kinds of symbolism attached to the snake. Firstly, as the enemy of man, it symbolises the powers of evil, but there is another kind of symbolism wherein, because it is the most subtle of all beasts, it is regarded as the emblem of the divine wisdom. "Be ye wise as serpents", refers, not to the craftiness of the devil, but to Divine Wisdom.

Thus the serpent on our apron denotes that we are encircled by the holy Wisdom. There is doubtless also a phallic significance, the serpent always being associated with that early form of worship, but in view of the late incorporation of this emblem on our regalia its phallic significance need not detain us.

We must not forget, however, that the serpent biting its tail and thus forming a circle has always been regarded as the emblem of eternity and more particularly of the Eternal Wisdom of God.

In conclusion it may be added that the snake is peculiarly associated with Shiva, whose close symbolic association with the 3rd degree has previously been stressed. After all, our own Bible tells us that it was by the serpent that death came into the world. Seeing that in the aprons of the 1st and 2nd degrees strings are used and the serpent omitted, this fact becomes peculiarly significant.

* * *

58. What do the substituted w..ds mean?

There is little doubt that the reason why there are two of these w..ds is that one of them was used by the "Ancients" and the other by the "Moderns," and at the Union it was agreed that both should be employed, so as to avoid any ill-feeling. Major Sanderson in "An Examination of the Masonic Ritual" points out that in their present form the first has no meaning in Hebrew, and the second is a proper name which occurs in the Old Testament. He believes that the latter was adopted because it was the only w...d in the authorised version resembling the original one. It is true that in the ritual we are given the w..ds and their meaning, but since neither as it stands can have the meaning indicated, it is evident that either the w..d having that meaning has become corrupt or that a wrong meaning has been given to the original w..d.

We have already pointed out that in several cases well-known Hebrew w..ds are wrongly translated, and it seems probable that the same thing has occurred here. There do exist Hebrew w..ds meaning "My Son is d..d" and also, "Alas, my son is d..d", but perhaps the most interesting discovery of Major Sanderson's is that there exist two tenses of an arabic verb which are identical with these two w..ds. Translated literally the one w..d means, "Not dying", and the other, "We do not die." With regard to the Hebrew w..ds, they would clearly refer to the Widow's son, and in "Who

Was Hiram Abiff" I have shown that H.A.B. is almost certainly merely a humanised form of Adonis, the Beloved of Astarte, her son and her husband, whose death she mourned annually, and further that symbolically Astarte is Mother Earth and Adonis the grain of corn which in one season is begotten by the earth and in the next is planted in the earth, dies but rises again at the harvest.

The Arabic interpretation reminds us of the words of the famous Athenian orator speaking of the Greek heroes, that dying thus, they died not. So this Arabic w..d spoken by the Master goes even further than our own, for it speaks of the resurrection and the life everlasting.

Nor need the presence of an Arabic w..d present any difficulty. Not only are mediæval magical rituals full of corrupt Arabic w..ds, but there has always been a tradition that the Crusades influenced Freemasonry. It is almost certain that the pointed arch, so characteristic of Gothic architecture, was copied by the European masons from the pointed arch of the Arabs. The wimple worn by women in the time of Henry II and Henry III is nothing but the veil worn by a Mahommedan woman, and that an appropriate Arabic w..d should work into the rituals of English Masons is far from surprising.

*   *   *

59. Who were Jubela, Jubelo and Jubelum?

These are the names given in the Scotch ritual to the three v...ns and are clearly symbolical. The full meaning of the words will be more intelligible to R. A. Masons, but their presence in the Scotch ritual is very significant.

In reality the names are made up of Jah, Bel, and Om, the names of the gods of Palestine, Phoenicia and Egypt, the word Om being the same as On, the title by which Isis invoked the dead Osiris. But more than this, the syllable at the end of each of the names, which is intended to distinguish the three villains, really constitutes the word AUM, our letter O more truly representing the pronunciation of the Hindu "U" than does the corresponding letter in English.

Therefore the v...ns represent a trinity of local Gods of whom, in the legends of the irrespective countries, both Baal (or Bel) and Om are fabled to have been slain. On the other hand, among the Hindus the letters AUM constitute the name of the All-Pervading. This word is considered to be a great word of power, which should never be pronounced aloud except by three persons in rotation, or under peculiar safeguards in the Temple. It symbolises the triune nature of the Deity, the letter "A" symbolising Brahma, the Creator; the letter "U,"

Vishnu, the Preserver, and the letter "M", Shiva, the Destroyer, and in the Scotch legend Jubelum is the third or last of the v...ns.

* * *

60. What is the meaning of A.L. on the 3rd Degree T.B.?

They represent the words *Anno Lucis*, or the year of Light, which means from the creation of the world. Masonically that event is reckoned to have been 4,000 B.C. It was Bishop Usher, one of the Prelates responsible for the authorised version of the Bible, who fixed on this date, or rather 4,004. In order to find the date of the Creation he added up the genealogies of our Lord and found that these covered a period of 4,004 years.

As Freemasonry under Anderson had definitely ceased to be Christian it was probably felt somewhat invidious to use the Christian era, hence this somewhat strange device, which consists of adding to the round number 4,000 the present year A.D., so that it would read 5,928.

The date on the T.B. refers to the supposed date of the death of our hero.

* * *

51. To what does the number 5, three times repeated, on the 3° T.B. refer?

Exoterically these figures refer to the three

groups of F.C.s who were sent in search, but they also have an esoteric meaning. The number 5 may be considered to represent the five senses in man, but man has not only a body but also a soul and a spirit, hence it is reasonable to argue that both soul and spirit have also their five senses: thus, corresponding to physical sight, would be clairvoyance. If they had not some such equivalent senses how could they function in the non-physical existence beyond the grave?

It will be remembered that one group of seekers entirely failed and these would represent our physical senses. The second company failed to find what they sought, but captured a group of criminals; the third group, representing the senses of the Spirit, actually found what all three sought. The meaning of the allegory is clear.

* * *

62. What is a Dormer Window?

Historically this is the hypostyle; the method by which Egyptian and Classical temples obtained light. The pillars of the central nave of such temples rose much higher than the roof of the aisles, thereby leaving an opening through which light entered the building. These, however, were many in number and it is difficult to justify the statement that there was only one such opening. It is probable therefore that the hypostyle and another opening have become confounded.

In temples dedicated to the Sun a hole was left in the roof so that a shaft of sunlight might fall on the altar at Noon, or at sunrise, on some special festival, such as the Summer or Winter Solstice. That this is what is intended seems to be indicated by the reference in our ritual to an annual festival at which special prayers were offered.

Symbolically the dormer window represents the means by which the Divine Light penetrates the deepest recesses of every man's nature.

CHAPTER IV.

PROBLEMS OF A MORE GENERAL NATURE.

63. Why is the Carpet checkered Black and white?

Symbolically to represent the journey of life, reminding us of alternate night and day and of the constant changes in men's fortunes, from sickness to health, from joy to sorrow, and ultimately from life to death.

* * *

64. On which side of the Chair is an Officer Invested?

If he is a P.M., on the South Side, to impress on the brethren the fact that he has already passed through the Chair of the Master. If he is not a P.M. he should be invested on the North side, implying thereby that he has still to pass through that Chair. The Master enters his chair on the North and leaves it by the South for the same reason that a candidate goes round the lodge by North, East, South and West.

* * *

65. Why do we go round the Lodge with the Sun and not across it?

In the Northern hemisphere the sun apparently rises in the East and passes round, via the South, to the West, and this symbolises life on earth. At night the sun was supposed to enter a kind of tunnel at the Western side of the world and pass through this tunnel back to the East, and the dead were supposed to accompany it in its boat.

As the lodge symbolises this world and man's life thereon, it is natural that we should go round with the course of the sun, for to go contrary to the sun, or to cut across the lodge as we please, would imply that we were dead, or ghosts.

There is, however, a working, the Emulation, which, while insisting that the cands. in the three degrees should go round with the sun, places no such restriction on other members of the lodge. Provided this freedom is restricted to those who have been r...d, quite a good case can be made out for it symbolically.

* * *

66. Should the S..n be given on passing the W.M.'s Chair after the Lodge is closed?

No, it is one of the s..ts and these having been locked up in a safe and sacred repository should not be taken out until the brethren proceed to open a new lodge.

* * *

67. Was there ever an Operative Grand Lodge?

Yes, and a fairly full description of it appears in an article by me in "Labour and Refreshment". It was called into existence by a lodge which met at *The Sign of the White Bear*, West Gate, Huddersfield, in 1832, the prime mover in the scheme being an Operative Mason called Thos. Fothergill. It included not only Masons but several other groups of allied trades, such as Carpenters and Joiners. Under the Masonic group were over 100 Lodges, containing at least 6,000 members. This Grand Lodge was in no way connected with any Speculative Grand Lodge and consisted entirely of genuine working Masons. It collapsed in 1835 after a great strike, this being the first strike in our modern sense of the word recorded in the history of the Craft.

* * *

68. Did these Operatives work a Ritual?

Yes, and certain details can be found among the documents in the possession of the Amalgamated Union of Building Trade Workers at their head office, where some of the old rituals survive.

The cands. had a very stringent obligation, were h.w., and the drama apparently dealt with a skeleton and the subject of death. Full details may be obtained from "Labour and Refreshment."*

*   *   *

68. What is a Firing Glass?

This is a specially made wine-glass constructed with a very heavy foot so that when a toast has been drunk the glass can be banged on the table without breaking. Quite a number of 18th century examples survive some of which can be seen in the Museum at Grand Lodge. A few lodges still use them and they can be obtained from most Masonic Furnishers. It is a great pity that all lodges do not keep up this old custom.

*   *   *

70. What is meant by the Secretary's Toast?

This is a very interesting old toast in honour of our Mother Lodge and presumably is so named because the Secretary of a lodge is supposed to know the name and number of the lodge in which every member has been initiated. It is not the Health of the Secretary. The procedure, which is peculiar, is as follows:—

W.M., Silence brethren, for the Secretary's toast.

Sec. (in a whisper to his left hand neighbour). Pass it on.

---

*See "Labour and Refreshment," publ. by the Baskerville Press, Ltd.

This sentence is then passed right round the table till it comes back to the Secretary from the right. He then says to his left hand neighbour, "What is it?"

This sentence is similarly passed round. Next he says, "A Mother of Masons," and when this is returned to him, whispers "How old is she?". When this returns to him the Secretary rises and, for the first time speaking aloud, calls out,

"Call it aloud, my mother is ——" (the No. of his l.) "I drink to my Mother Lodge". He drinks and resumes his seat.

The brother on his left then rises, does not repeat the rest of the sentence, but only calls out the number of his mother lodge, drinks and resumes his seat, and so, in rotation, until it has come back to the brother on the immediate right of the Secretary.

Then the latter raises his firing glass and strikes once on the table. The brother on his left follows him, and so each in turn, till it comes back to the Secretary. Twice more this knock goes round in rotation and when the brother on the right of the Secretary has knocked for the third time, the latter, and all the brethren in unison, in time with him, give the roll fire, thrice. This is given by grinding the base of the firing glass with a circular motion three times on the table. This done, the firing glasses are raised once more in the air and brought down altogether in one tremendous crash. This is called, "On the crest of the wave," and ends the fire. Note, there is no "point, left" etc., in this toast.

Strictly this toast should be given even before the King's toast, but very often it is given after the Toast of the Grand Master, but before that of the Grand Officers.

* * *

71. What are the Chivalric Degrees?

These are advanced grades which lie beyond the Craft and the Arch. They include *The Knights Templar* and *The Knights of St. John of Malta*, which work under Grand Priory, whose Headquarters are at Mark Mason's Hall. They carry on the traditions of those famous Mediæval Orders and symbolically represent the life of the Christian and his war with the world. They are great Grades, with many valuable lessons to teach, and are restricted to professing Christians, the ob. being taken on the Holy Trinity. To the same group belong the Red Cross of Constantine, which degree qualifies a brother for admission to the Order of *The Knights of St. John and the Holy Sepulchre*. This too has its Headquarters at Mark Mason's Hall.

The third group is *The Royal Order of Scot-*

land, which works two degrees, *The Harodim* and *The Rosy Cross*. This order is peculiar in that there can exist only one Grand Lodge in all the world, whose seat is at Edinburgh. In England the degrees are conferred in Provincial Grand Lodges. Like the other degrees it is a Christian Order. The *Rosy Cross* must not be confounded with the *Rose Croix*, which is the 18th degree of the A. & A. Rite. This is a Hermetic, and not a Chivalric, degree and is worked under charters granted by the Supreme Council, whose Headquarters are at 10, Duke Street, London W.

*   *   *

72. Can you give me a list of all the Degrees now working in England?

Excluding the six Chivalric degrees already mentioned, they are as follows:—

The three Craft degrees and the *Royal Arch*, which are controlled by Grand Lodge.

The A. & A. Rite, which works the following degrees:—18th or *Rose Croix of Heredom*. 30th 31st, 32nd and 33rd degrees, the latter four being as a rule only worked at 10, Duke Street, London.

The Secret Monitor, which works two degrees and a Chair degree and has its own Supreme Conclave. This body also controls the seven degrees of the Scarlet Cord.

Then, of course, there is Mark Grand Lodge, which controls the two Mark degrees, *Mark Man* and *Mark Master* and also the *Royal Ark Mariner*. At Mark Mason's Hall are also the Headquarters of the Cryptic and the Allied Degrees. The former may be considered as pendants of the *Royal Arch* and consist of *The Most Excellent Master, the Royal, Select* and *Super-Excellent Masters*. The *Excellent Master* which consists of passing the four veils, and in Scotland is always given prior to the *Royal Arch* degree, is not the same as the *Most Excellent Master*. In England it is worked at Bristol, and in one or two places in the North but, strange to say, it is not under the control of Grand Chapter.

The Allied Degrees consist of *St. Lawrence, the Martyr*; *The Knight of Constantinople*; *The Red Cross of Babylon*; *The Grand High Priest*; *The Grand Tyler of King Solomon* and *The Secret Monitor*. It will be noticed that it is possible to obtain the Secret Monitor under two distinct Grand Lodges, but the Allied Degrees give only the first degree, and there is a working arrangement between Grand Conclave and the Allied Degrees that the first degree of the Secret Monitor taken under the auspices of either body shall be recognised by the other.

At Newcastle are the Headquarters of *The Royal Arch Knight Templar Priest*, which is really the Supreme Degree of a whole series which, like the intermediate degrees of the Ancient and Accepted Rite, are only conferred by name.

At Bradford is the Headquarters of *The Illustrious Order of Light*; there is also the *Soc. Ros. in Anglia*, which works nine grades, and finally, we must not forget the *Cork Degree*, which has its own board of Grand Corks.

It will thus be seen that the brother who is anxious to take additional degrees in Freemasonry has no lack of choice.

*   *   *

73. Who was the First Grand Master of Freemasons?

Anthony Sayer, who was chosen Grand Master at an Assembly of Free and Accepted Masons held at the Goose and Gridiron on St. John the Baptist's Day, 1717. He subsequently lost all his money in the South Sea Bubble and was one of the first brethren to receive assistance from the Benevolent Fund. Towards the close of his life he was glad to serve as Grand Tyler.

*   *   *

74. What is meant by a peculiar system of Morality?

I suggest that originally the text read, "A peculiar system or morality." In the middle ages a morality was the term used to describe a religious play, such as those which were constantly given by the various Guilds. If we accept this interpretation it does exactly describe each of our degrees, which should be compared with the old morality, "Everyman," which by allegory and symbol dealt with the death of every man.

* * *

75. What is meant by the extended working of the I.M.?

This is part of the secret working of the Installation of a Master. Whereas in the ordinary Emulation form only a small part, taken from the centre of the ceremony, is given, and the Board of Installed Masters is opened by *Authority*, in the extended working the Master elect, as in the other Craft Degrees, is entrusted, the Board of Installed Masters is then opened in full, the Master elect is re-admitted and the ceremony worked in full, after which there is a complete Closing ceremony. This ceremony is largely used in the Provinces although to a considerable extend it has died out in London. Recently there was a lengthy discussion in Grand Lodge as to whether the extended working was an authorised ceremony and after mature consideration Grand Lodge definitely decided that it was.

* * *

76. What are the Ancient Charges?

The total number of the Ancient Charges and Constitutions is about 78 and they all appear to be copies of still earlier documents. They belong to the Operative period, before the formation of Grand Lodge, and the earliest is known as the *Regius MS.*, which was unearthed by James Halliwell in 1839. It is believed to date from 1390 and is a curious mixture, including early legends of the Craft and the Charges given to an Apprentice when he was indentured.

In the Charges are much of the groundwork which was afterwards expanded into the moral lectures that we find in our present rituals. Of the legends some, such as the two pillars erected by Jabal and Jubal, whereon was inscribed all knowledge, have become the basis of certain of the advanced degrees. We also get a tangled mass of references to Hermes, Euclid and Pythagoras, and of course to King Solomon. Their chief importance lies in the fact that despite their early date they indicate that even in the 14th century there was a Speculative side to Freemasonry.

* * *

77. At the Banquet may a Junior Brother call up a Senior?

Strictly, no, but a certain freedom of inter-

pretation is permissible. No brother below the
Chair should call up a Past Master, he must
wait until the Past Master calls him up, and no
Past Master may call up a Grand Officer. It is
generally acknowledged, however, that the
reigning Master in his own lodge may call up
anyone.

Although some sticklers for etiquette claim
that an ordinary member of the rank and file
should not call up any officer of the lodge, in
most lodges this is not insisted on and it is
quite usual to call up even the Wardens.

*   *   *

CHAPTER V.

HISTORICAL PROBLEMS.

78. Of what interest to Masons are the Initiation Rites of the Savages?

Some Masonic writers consider that what we now call Freemasonry dates its origin from the primitive initiation rites of a boy into manhood and that therefore examples of these rites, which still survive among the native Australian, African and Red Indian races, throw a flood of light on the origin and meaning of many obscure parts of our rituals.

Among these primitive people, when a boy reaches puberty he has to pass through elaborate rites of initiation to prepare him for manhood. Therein he is taught whence he comes, his duty to his tribe, the traditions of the tribe and that he must die, but that death does not end all.

Many of these ceremonies include the symbolical slaying of the candidate and his being raised from the grave. Good examples occur among some of the Australian tribes, in New Guinea, and among the Yao people in Nyasaland. During these ceremonies certain signs well-known to Masons are employed.

The School of Masonic students to which we

have referred consider that these initiation rites ultimately developed into the Ancient Mysteries which played such an important part in the days of Greece and Rome.

* * *

79. What were the Ancient Mysteries?

In Ancient Egypt, Greece and Rome, in addition to the exoteric worship of the gods there existed the Mysteries. Whereas among the primitive savages *all* boys had to be initiated, at the period we are now considering only a percentage of the population entered the Mysteries, for which indeed certain qualifications were laid down. For example, candidates for the Eleusinian Mysteries had to be free born Greeks, whose hands were clear of blood and who were of good moral character.

In the Mysteries the candidates were taught by means of allegories and symbols certain doctrines not revealed to the outside world. There was usually a legend of some divine hero who died and rose from the dead, and the candidates re-enacted this legend, symbolically passing through the Underworld and being ultimately brought back from the grave possessed of certain secrets, among which was the knowledge that behind all the gods there existed really only One God. There were also secret signs and passwords.

* * *

ATTIS, THE HERO OF THE MYSTERY RITE
OF CYBELE.

80. Which were the four Chief Mysteries?

They were the Mystery of Eleusis, which told of the descent of Persephone into Hades, and the search for her by her mother, Ceres, who ultimately brought her back to the light of day. This was the Mystery Rite of Greece.

The Egyptian Mysteries are generally spoken of as "The Mystery of Isis." Apparently it had several degrees and its main theme was the death and resurrection of Osiris.

The third Mystery was that of Cybele. It told of the death of Attis, sometimes called Adonis, and the grief of his mother, Cybele, sometimes called Astarte. The latter was both his mother and his wife.

This was the great cult of Asia. In Babylon Astarte was known as Ishtar and Adonis as Damuzi. In Syria and Palestine Damuzi became Tammuz, and later, was called by the name *Adonis*, which is the same word as *Adonai* and means, *Lord*.

The fourth Mystery Cult is that of Mithra, which originated in Persia but was taken up by the Roman army and became the great Cult of the legions. In like manner Mithra was slain and rose from the dead, but whereas the other three cults seemed to have been a dramatic representation of the planting of the corn, which dies when planted and rises again as a bountiful harvest, Mithra seems to have symbolised the Sun, which dies each night and rises again the next day.

* * *

81. Is Freemasonry connected with any of these Mysteries?

Freemasonry has such obvious similarities both in its teaching and in its *modus operandi* that almost all students are agreed that it is at any rate the spiritual heir of the Ancient Mysteries. A considerable number of students go further, however, and consider that it is definitely descended from one or other of them. Some consider that the Egyptian Mystery is the parent, but the author believes that Freemasonry is descended from the Syrian form of the Cult of Astarte and Tammuz.*

As all these four Cults came to Rome, where they borrowed freely from each other, it is quite probable that both Egypt and Greece have also helped to form our present rituals.

* * *

82. What were the Roman Colleges of Architects?

In the time of the Romans the various trades were organised into Guilds of Colleges, the Masons being under the control of the Colleges of Architects which had their lodges in all the chief cities of the Roman Empire. Each of

---

*For further details see "Who Was Hiram Abiff," by Ward. Publ. by the Baskerville Press, Ltd.

these Guilds, including the Architects, had their own special cult, and at Pompeii the ruins of their lodge room exist, wherein was discovered a mosaic table-top, corresponding somewhat to our Masonic Tracing Board. Thereon was inlaid a combined square, level and plumb rule, a skull, and certain other emblems which clearly indicate a drama of death and resurrection. In the wall of the same building is a carved stone whereon are depicted the various tools of a Mason, compasses, square, maul, etc., and above all, an up-turned urn. Among the Romans the dead were not buried but burnt, and their ashes deposited in a sepulchral urn. The fact that the urn is upturned implies that the ashes of the dead have been scattered to the four cardinal points of heaven. Hence, these two relics prove that the Roman Colleges of Architects had during their initiation ceremonies a dramatic representation of death and resurrection.

* * *

83. Who were the Comacine Masons?

On the downfall of the Roman Empire the Guild system was shattered by the barbarians, but one College of Architects survived at Comacina, a fortified island in the middle of Lake Como. In due course the Lombards, who obtained control of North Italy, began to realise the desirability of order and civilisation.

At that time their king, Rothares, issued an edict, on Nov. 22nd 643 A.D., confirming the privileges of this college and giving them control over all the Masons in his kingdom of North Italy.

Thus encouraged, they spread rapidly through North Italy into South Germany and France, and from the place of their origin became known as *Comacine Masons*. Their work is easily recognisable by the appearance of the endless knot and the Lion of Judah.

When St. Augustine came to convert the English, he brought with him members of this fraternity, who are here called, *Liberi Muratori*, which when translated means, simply, *Freemasons*; while Paulinus, who was sent to convert North England, is spoken of as *Magister*, a technical phrase implying that he was himself a Master Mason of the Comacines. Hence it seems clear that the later Freemasons were directly descended from the Comacines, who had themselves descended from the old Roman College of Architects at Comacina.

*   *   *

84. When was the word Freemason first used?

The actual word Freemason first occurs in "The History of the Company of Masons of the City of London" in 1375, that is to say, some

fifteen years after the use of English replaced
that of French in the English Law Courts.

* * *

85. Who were the Guild Masons?

During the Middle Ages there were two distinct groups of Masons, the Comacine Masons,
who in England became known as Freemasons,
and the Guild Masons. The former had a
monopoly of ecclesiastical building and were
free to go from place to place and build
Churches and Abbeys anywhere, therein being
markedly different from the Guild Masons.
These were the local builders in each town, who
constructed the houses of the town and had a
monopoly of all building in their mother city,
for which privilege they paid by keeping the
city walls in repair. They were not allowed,
however, to go from one town to another, each
town having its own Guild, which claimed a
monopoly of work in that town.

But on the other hand, they were not permitted to build any large ecclesiastical edifice,
except when employed by a proper Guild of
Freemasons. If a church or a monastery re-
quired building, a lodge of Freemasons was
called in, who established on the spot a tem-
porary lodge room and undertook the work,
contracting with the Abbot or Bishop to build
a certain sized building for a specified sum.

Apparently very often they hired the local Guild masons to do the less important work, such as squaring the ashlars, always, however, retaining in their own hands the planning, carving and more complex stone-cutting.

In short, the Freemasons were a national, almost an international, body and better educated than the Guild Masons, who were restricted to a definite locality. It is from the Freemasons we claim descent, but the Guild Masons may be represented by the few Operative lodges which still survive.

* * *

86. Who are the Companionage?

These were the French form of the English Freemasons or, in other words, when with the growth of nationalism the Comacines ceased to be international, their members in France became known as *The Companionage*, just as in Germany they became known as *The Stein-Metzen*.

It should be noted, however, that the Companionage, like the English Operative Grand Lodge of 1832, included a number of Allied Trades as well as Stone Masons. They were divided into three great groups, each of which recognised a traditional chief, who was the hero of a legend and was supposed to have conferred a charge on his followers. Each division called its members the Sons of this Chief, namely, the *Sons of Solomon*, the *Sons of Maître Jacques* and the *Sons of Maître Soubise*. Of these the *Sons of Solomon* were acknowledged to be the oldest. Perdiguier, who is our chief authority, and was himself a Son of Solomon, acknowledges that this group had the Hiramic legend, but he gives us little information, telling us more of the reputed founders of the other two branches. We learn that Jacques and Soubise at first swore an oath of blood brotherhood, but later quarrelled and ultimately Jacques was murdered by the followers of Soubise, having been betrayed to them by one of his own disciples. The legend bears striking similarities to the Hiramic tale and also to the Gospel account of the death of Christ. Some of the ceremonies of the Companionage are very similar to those familiar to Rose Croix Masons.

* * *

87. What is the difference between an Accepted and an Entered Freemason?

We gather from John Aubrey that an *Entered Apprentice* was an Operative Freemason who passed through the usual seven years' apprenticeship, at the end of which time he was qualified to work as a Mason, whereas an *Accepted Mason* was what we should now call a *Speculative*, namely, one who was accepted into a lodge of freemasons although he had never had the proper training as an apprentice and neither was able, nor intended, to work as an Operative mason. It was from the *Acceptance*, so-called, that modern Freemasonry developed, it being the Accepted Masons who took the leading part in the foundation of Grand Lodge.

* * *

88. Who was the first Speculative Mason in England of whom we have any record?

On May 20th, 1641, Robert Moray, "General Quarter Master of the Armie of Scotland," was initiated at Newcastle by members of the lodge of Edinburgh who were with the Scottish army which, as a result of the Bishop's War, had entered England in arms against King Charles I. This is actually the earliest surviving record of the initiation of a Speculative Freemason in England, but it should be noted that he was a Scotsman and initiated in a Scotch lodge, although it was meeting on English soil. However, at 4.30 on October 16th, 1646, Elias Ashmole, the Founder of the Ashmolean Museum at Oxford, was initiated at Warrington, Lancashire, and at the same time Colonel Henry Mainwaring was initiated. Although these are the first two Englishmen of whose initiation as Speculatives we have a record, students who have examined the wills of the various men who according to Ashmole were present when he was initiated, have discovered that every one of them must have been Accepted or Speculative Masons.

* * *

89. Who were the founders of Grand Lodge?

According to the Book of Constitutions issued by Dr. James Anderson in 1738, four lodges which met in London held a joint meeting at *The Apple Tree Tavern*, Charles Street, Covent Garden. This was in 1716, and at that meeting they decided "to revive the Quarterly Communication of the Officers of Lodges (called the Grand Lodge)". They resolved to hold an annual meeting and feast, and this took place on St. John the Baptist Day, 1717, at the *Goose and Gridiron Alehouse*, in St. Paul's Churchyard. Here they elected Anthony Sayer as Grand Master and Mr. Jacob Lamball, Carpenter, and Captain Joseph Elliot, as Grand Wardens.

* * *

90. Who were the chief Leaders in this movement?

In addition to Sayer, Dr. Anderson, a Presbyterian Scotch Minister; John, Second Duke of Montague; Payne and especially Desaguliers, seem to have been the moving spirits.

* * *

91. Was it Opposed?

Yes, first of all many of the more conserva-
tive masons, particularly those who were genuine Operatives, resented what they regarded
as an innovation and an attempt to take away
the independence of the individual lodges.
Secondly, by issuing their Book of Constitutions, the first edition of which appeared in
1723, Grand Lodge brought its existence before
the eyes of the general public, many of whom
thought it a suitable subject for ridicule. But
the most serious hostility came from the Church
of Rome. This followed on its introduction
into France and in 1738 Clement XII published
a Bull condemning Freemasonry. Previous to
this in England the opposition generally took
the form of burlesquing the Freemasons, and
one body which came into existence apparently
for this particular purpose was called *The
Gormogons*.

*   *   *

92. What was The Grand Lodge of York?

In the North of England there were many
Operative Lodges which, like the lodges in
London, had by this time admitted non-Opera-
tive masons, or as we should call them, Speculatives. In particular there was a very famous
one at York and this, seeing the success of the
Grand Lodge in London, proclaimed itself a

Grand Lodge, in the year 1725. It received the submission of a number of North country lodges and, strange to say, always seems to have been in friendly relations with the Grand Lodge at London. After varying vicissitudes it finally collapsed in 1791 and its constituent lodges soon after joined the United Grand Lodge of England.

* * *

93. When did Freemasonry cease to be purely Christian?

In 1723. Before that date, as is clear from the Ancient Charges, Masons were charged to be true to Holy Church and hold no form of heresy, while prayers to the Trinity also occurred.

In 1721 the New Grand Master, the Duke of Montague, felt that the old charges were inadequate and instructed Dr. Anderson to make a digest of them, so as to form them into a better set of regulations for the lodges. Dr. Anderson, assisted by a committee of 14 brethren, completed his work and the book was published in 1723. Here, after admitting that in ancient days Masons were charged to be of the religion of the country in which they lived, it was declared that this was no longer necessary. The actual clause, although somewhat vague, has always been understood to imply that a Mason must believe in God, but without making any attempt to define what is meant by that word.   At that date Deism was popular among the educated classes, due to a reaction from the bitter religious controversies of the 17th century.

      *   *   *

94. Were the Grand Lodges of Scotland and Ireland derived from England ?

No, they were each formed independently out of ancient lodges in their own territory who copied the example of the four London Lodges.   The Grand Lodge of Ireland was founded in 1725 and that of Scotland in 1736.

      *   *   *

95.   Which is the oldest Grand Lodge founded abroad?

The Grand Lodge of France, founded in 1736 out of lodges which had been originally started by the Grand Lodge of England.   The present Grand Orient is the successor of this, the oldest daughter Grand Lodge of England.

      *   *   *

96.   What is meant by the Grand Lodges of the Ancients and Moderns?

About 1753 a large number of Masons, dissatisfied with the conduct of the original Grand Lodge of England, set up a new Grand Lodge, claiming to be guardians of the *ancient* traditions of the Order. Their chief cause of complaint was an allegation that the original Grand Lodge had made numerous innovations. There seems to have been some justification for this charge, since it appears that, owing to the publication of several exposures of Freemasonry, Grand Lodge had reversed the words and p.w.s., and probably also the Signs, of the first and second degrees, so as to prevent anyone who had read one of these exposures succeeding in obtaining entry into a lodge by means of the information thus illegally procured. There were doubtless also personal reasons, and it seems as if some of the moving spirits were Irish Masons settled in London, who owed no allegiance to the English Grand Lodge. Be that as it may, this new Grand Lodge dubbed its opponents *The Moderns* and took for itself the title of *Ancients*. The Ancients were strong champions of the higher degrees, on which the Moderns frowned.

* * *

97. How was the Feud between the two Healed?

After half a century of bitter controversy, better feelings prevailed, and in 1809 committees were formed to explore avenues of reunion. This was finally effected at a Grand Lodge of Reconciliation held on St. John the Baptist Day in 1813.

Delegates from 641 Modern and 359 Ancient Lodges met and were so mingled together as to be indistinguishable one from the other. The two Grand Masters both took their seats in the East and then one of them resigned, and the Duke of Sussex, Grand Master of the Moderns, was unanimously elected by all the delegates as Grand Master of *The United Grand Lodge of England*.

*   *   *

98. Has this struggle left its Traces in Modern Freemasonry?

Yes, it was ended in a compromise and one of the results has been that certain conditions then laid down have ever since been regarded as unalterable. Of these perhaps the most important, and certainly the most equivocal, is the statement that Freemasonry consists of three degrees and three degrees only, *including* the Holy Royal Arch. The phrase is equivocal because the Royal Arch is *not* included in the three degrees; its meetings take place in an entirely separate body, known as the *Chapter*, and every M.M. applying for admission to that degree has to be balloted for and elected. Were the Royal Arch really part of the third degree, every M.M. should automatically go on to it, without having to be balloted for, as is the case with the F.C. and M.M..

Another unfortunate effect was the unsatisfactory condition in which the so-called Higher Degrees were left. At the beginning of the 19th century an attempt was made to wipe these out of existence. Fortunately the attempt failed, and to-day they are practically and tacitly recognised, but even still officially, Grand Lodge knows nothing of them.

The different workings of the ritual which are to be found in various lodges also bear witness to the old struggle. Some lodges inheriting their rituals from the "Ancients" and others from the "Moderns."

*   *   *

99. What is the difference between a District and a Provincial Grand Lodge?

Provincial Grand Lodges constitute the subdivisions of Freemasonry inside England, but overseas these similar divisions are called "District Grand Lodges" and the District Grand Master has slightly wider powers than the Provincial Grand Master. This is of course due to the fact that he is separated by considerable distance from the Head Offices of Grand Lodge and therefore cannot be expected to refer details to Great Queen Street, seeing that he would have to wait much longer for an answer than would a Provincial Grand Master.

*   *   *

100. Why is the Grand Lodge of England not in Fraternal Relations with the Grand Orient of France?

In France, owing to the Papal Bull which forbade Roman Catholics to be Freemasons, only men who have broken with the dominant religion of the country can be members of a Masonic Lodge. In that country there are very few Protestants and the opposition to the dominant form of the Christian religion consists largely of Agnostics. These gradually drifted into open hostility, not only towards Roman Catholicism, but to practically any form of religion whatsoever. They also began to mix in politics. Finally, in 1876 they eliminated the Name of T.G.A.O.T.U. from their rituals and declared that belief in God was not an essential qualification for admission into Freemasonry.

The Grand Lodge of England considered this to be a removal of one of the ancient landmarks and immediately broke off fraternal relations.

* * *

101. What is the Difference between an Operative and a Speculative Freemason?

An Operative Freemason is one who actually cuts stone and builds buildings, whereas a Speculative Freemason is one who, although he is not a Builder, uses building terms and tools as symbols and allegories for teaching mystical or moral lessons.

Modern Freemasonry, as ruled by the Grand Lodge of England, is purely Speculative, giving no practical instruction in Building Trade secrets, although it includes among its members not only architects but men who earn their living as Operative masons.

INDEX.

HOW TO MAKE A GOOD MASONIC SPEECH.

A COURSE OF SIX LECTURES

By Wor. Bro. J. S. M. WARD, M.A.

WHO has not felt that terrible SINKING FEELING which assails even an experienced Mason when unexpectedly called upon to make a SPEECH at the BANQUET, and what Warden has not looked forward with dismay to the long list of Toasts which he will have to propose when he becomes Master of the Lodge?

The real difficulty is that whereas every conscientious mason spends considerable time in mastering the ritual, few of them have had the opportunity of learning how to make a speech, and it is to supply this need that this School of Masonic After-Dinner Speaking has been inaugurated.

METHOD OF INSTRUCTION.

This is conducted on the lines of a Correspondence School. The course consists of a series of six lectures wherein are set out the general principles which should be followed in all after-dinner speaking, precise instructions how to prepare a speech, together with examples of complete speeches suitable for various occasions. There are, in addition, a number of outline speeches, which will encourage the student to compose for himself speeches in his own words on definite lines.

The Lectures are despatched monthly: the fee for the complete course being only **One Guinea**, which should be sent to The Baskerville Press, 161 New Bond Street, London, W.1.

THE MASONIC HANDBOOK SERIES

J. S. M. WARD, M.A., F.S.S., P.M.

With an INTRODUCTION by The Hon. Sir John Cockburn, M.D., K.C.M.G., P.G.D., P.Dep. G.M. South Australia.

Size 6ins. x 4½ins.   Price 2s. 6d. net each.

1. THE E.A.'s HANDBOOK.

Contents. The Opening—The Tyler—Preparation—Admission—The Orb.—The Sn., T. and W.—The Charge—Closing.

This useful little book gives a simple but scientific explanation of the inner meaning of the 1st degree.

"This little book . . . . supplies what has long been felt to be a need in Masonic symbolic teaching."

The Masonic Record.

2. THE F.C's HANDBOOK.

Contents. Preparation—P.W.—Opening—Preliminary Steps—The S.ts—The Conclusion of the Ceremony—Tracing Board—Closing.

"Students of mature initiation, will do well to consider and reconsider the 2°, ... in the light of the dormer which Bro. Ward . . . has opened upon it."

The Times Literary Supplement.

3. THE M.M.'s BOOK.

Contents. Question and P.W.—The Opening—The Symbolical Journeys—The Exhortation—The S.ts—The Badge—The Legend—Tracing Board, etc.—Closing—Conclusion.

"These neat little publications . . . show in simple language that the Masonic Craft is not only a world-wide civilising medium . . . but a mine of wealth in which much of the wisdom of the ages has become embedded."

The Sydney Daily Telegraph.

The Masonic Handbook Series

(Continued.)

---

4. AN OUTLINE HISTORY OF FREEMASONRY.

By J. S. M. WARD, M.A., P.M.

with an INTRODUCTION by The Rt. Hon. F. Pollock, Bt., P.Dept.G.Reg.

Well Illustrated. **Price 3s. net.**

Contents.—The Primitive Beginnings—The Mysteries—The Comacine Masons—Mediæval Freemasons—The Formation of Grand Lodge—"Ancients and Moderns."

This well illustrated book traces the evolution of Freemasonry from pre-historic times down to the present day.

5. THE HIGHER DEGREES HANDBOOK,

By J. S. M. WARD, M.A., P.M., P.Z., P.M.W.S.

Well Illustrated. Price 3s. net.

CONTENTS. Historical Survey—The Mark Degree—The Holy R.A.—The Cryptic degrees—Ancient and Accepted Rite—Royal Order of Scotland—Knights Templar—Knights of Malta—Remaining Degrees.

A book which should be in the possession of every M.M. as it gives a brief account of all the degrees beyond the Craft and will help him in his search for further light.

6. THE MORAL TEACHINGS OF FREEMASONRY.

(With which is incorporated Masonic Proverbs, Poems and Sayings).
By Wors. Bro. J. S. M. WARD, M.A.

Price 3s. nett. Ready Oct., 1926.

In response to numerous requests Bro. Ward has written this volume as the sixth of his famous series. As its title suggests, it deals with those fundamental moral teachings of the Craft which have made it universally respected even by men outside our Order.

In it is incorporated "Masonic Proverbs, Poems and Sayings." Thus this book may be regarded as a handy compendium of Masonic Morality, and will prove a most acceptable present to either a newly raised Brother or an old and experienced P.M.

The Magic of Freemasonry.

By Maj. A. E. POWELL.

F'cap 8vo. cloth.   7s. 6d. net.

A most inspiring book which deals in a new and original way with the meaning of Craft Masonry. The explanation of the inner meaning of the W.T.s in each degree herein given would alone be sufficient to justify its inclusion in every Masonic library.

An Examination of the Masonic Ritual.

BY

W. BRO. MAJ. M. SANDERSON.

F'cap. 8vo. Cloth.   Third and Enlarged Edition.
Illustrated.   6s. nett.

The author is a profound student of the Egyptian Mysteries and of various initiatory Rites of Primitive Races. Himself an initiate of some of the latter, he has been able to learn therefrom many facts which throw a flood of light on the History of our Order and the meaning of our Ceremonies.

An Explanation of the Royal Arch Degree.

BY Ex. COMP. J. S. M. WARD, M.A., P.Z.

Crown 8vo.   Cloth 5s. net. Fully Illustrated.

As a result of the numerous requests received by the author to follow up his books on the meaning of the Craft by one explaining this Supreme Degree, he herein supplies a key to the whole ceremony and gives a clear interpretation of this highly mystical degree.

TOLD THROUGH THE AGES

BY

Wors. Bro. J. S. M. WARD, M.A., P.M., P.Z.

Fully Illus.   Demy 8vo.   Price 10s. 6d. nett;

This book marks an ENTIRELY NEW DEPARTURE in Masonic Literature. It contains twenty enthralling short stories, each representing a distinct epoch in the evolution of the human race. Each episode depicts some phase of what we now call Freemasonry and shows the influence for good of its teaching. The allegories reveal a hidden significance which will astonish and delight the reader by the very element of surprise which throughout dominates the series.

In these stories we are present at the Willing Sacrifice of Great Heart in the dawn of history and learn of what befell the first man who invented the Keystone in the days of the Pharaohs. We witness the tragic end of the Substitute King in Babylon and the Passing of the College of Architects at Pompeii. We hear how three Masons discovered a Secret Vault while rebuilding the Abbey of St. Albans, and of the prominent part John the Mason played in saving the Abbey of Tewkesbury, together with many more inspiring stories which teach the lesson that amid the apparent turmoil and chaos of the world there is a Divine Providence ever leading mankind towards the Light.

LESSING'S MASONIC DIALOGUES

BY

THE REV. DR. A. COHEN, M.A.

PAST GRAND CHAPLAIN OF WARWICKSHIRE.

Price 6s. nett.   F'cap.   Post Free 6s. 2d.

Although Lessing lived nearly 150 years ago, this is the first time that a full and accurate translation of his important Masonic work has appeared in England in book form. Lessing herein sets forth his lofty ideals of Freemasonry, and his message will be read with profound interest and sympathy by all thoughtful Masons.

The valuable notes appended to the original work by the gifted translator considerably enhance the utility of the book. Dr. Cohen is widely known and respected, not only in Warwickshire, but throughout the whole country, as a man who may well be called an "Apostle of Freemasonry."

The Sign Language of the Mysteries

By Wors. Bro. J. S. M. WARD, M.A.
P.M., P.Z., P.M.W.S.

Illustrated in Colour and Gold.   In 2 Vols.   *Crown Quarto.*
Sepia and Black and White.   Price £4 4s.
Edition limited to 1,000 numbered copies.

More than 500 EXAMPLES of the APPROPRIATE USE of SIGNS, etc., WELL KNOWN to MASONS are quoted in this book, yet although the significance of these facts will be evident to every Mason who reads these volumes, the author has been careful so to write that no one outside our Order can pentrate that veil of secrecy which has always been considered binding on Freemasons.

The subject is dealt with in a thoroughly scientific manner and the author not only PROVES that these SIGNS have DESCENDED to us from our ancestors by a regular succession, but also indicates their full symbolic meaning.

The Symbolism of the Gods of the Egyptians and the Light They Throw on Freemasonry

BY
DR. T. M. STEWART, P.M., 33°, U.S.A.

Fully Illustrated.
Price 10s. 6d. nett.   Post Free 10s. 10d.

Dr. T. M. Stewart is well known in the United States as one of the most interesting lecturers on Symbolism and the Ancient Wisdom. In this book he has produced a most valuable contribution to a clear interpretation of the Ancient Egyptian System of Symbolic teaching, and shows how it throws a flood of light on Freemasonry.

The book Dr. Stewart has written will prove of the utmost value to Masonic students, the more so as he has devoted a special chapter on the subject, to which, as a member of the 33°, he is peculiarly qualified to speak.

THE HUNG SOCIETY OF CHINA

(Showing its close relation with Freemasonry).

BY

Wors. Bro. J. S. M. Ward, M.A., and Bro. W. G. Stirling.

The Hung Society works a TRULY MAGNIFICENT RITUAL, which on the one hand THROWS A FLOOD OF LIGHT on the ANCIENT MYSTERIES and on the other has STRIKING ANALOGIES WITH MODERN FREEMASONRY.

This work shows that this similarity is not ACCIDENTAL, for the bulk of the SIGNS used are WELL KNOWN to MASONS, and the ceremony itself is so similar as to indicate that the Hung League, or TRIAD SOCIETY, and FREEMASONRY must be derived from a common ancestor. The root matter of CRAFT, MARK and ARCH, of K.T., ROSE CROIX, and, above all, the ROYAL ORDER OF SCOTLAND, pass before our eyes in this sublime Chinese ritual.

These facts have enabled Bro. Ward, while ostensibly explaining the Hung Ceremony, to do a like service for similar incidents in Freemasonry, without disclosing Masonic secrets to those outside the Order.

The ritual is translated and printed in full, which has never been done before, and is explained in elaborate notes, while the rubrics are printed in red, thus greatly facilitating study.

VOLUME 1.

This contains the COMPLETE RITUAL, now for the first time laid before the public. It is printed in black, with the rubrics in red, and is fully annotated.

VOLUME 2.

This deals with the FRAMEWORK OF THE DEGREE, which depicts the journey of the Soul through the Underworld to Heaven. When our readers have finished this volume they will understand why Freemasonry is similar not only to the Hung Society, but to other secret Societies which exist all over the world.

VOLUME 3.

This explains the various Magical details in the ceremony and gives a complete allegorical and mystical interpretation of the whole degree.

Three Vols.   Printed in Red and Black.   Price £6 6s. the Set.

Copiously illustrated in colour and black and white.

Edition limited to 1,500 numbered sets.

Printed in the United States
116998LV00003B/100/A